For my mother and Mike
and in memory of my father

Contents

Acknowledgements

I would like to thank Abdulrazak Gurnah for his rigorous supervision of my doctoral thesis which led eventually to this study. Together with John Thieme and Lyn Innes he provided valuable comments on sections of the manuscript. Katherine Frank has always been ready with much-needed encouragement of my work in some difficult times. Above all, I am indebted to Mike Sanders for the intellectual and emotional support that makes everything – not just writing – possible.

I am grateful to the following publishers and journals for permission to reprint, in whole or in part, work which has previously been published: *Journal of Commonwealth Literature* for permission to reprint material from 'Rehearsing Voices: Salman Rushdie's *Grimus*', 27:1 (1992), 128–38; *Wasafiri* for permission to reprint material from 'Rushdie's Women', 18 (1993), 13–17; Rodopi, Amsterdam for permission to reprint 'Through Childhood's Window: *Haroun and the Sea of Stories*' from M. D. Fletcher (ed.), *Reading Rushdie: Perspectives on the Fiction of Salman Rushdie*, Cross/Cultures 16 (1994), 335–41.

Series editor's foreword

Contemporary World Writers is an innovative new series of authoritative introductions to a range of culturally diverse contemporary writers from outside Britain and the United States, or from 'minority' backgrounds within Britain or the United States. In addition to providing comprehensive general introductions, books in the series also argue stimulating original theses, often but not always related to contemporary debates in post-colonial studies.

The series locates individual writers within their specific cultural contexts, while recognising that such contexts are themselves invariably a complex mixture of hybridised influences. It aims to counter tendencies to appropriate the writers discussed into the canon of English or American literature or to regard them as 'other'.

Each volume includes a chronology of the writer's life, an introductory section on formative contexts and intertexts, discussion of all the writer's major works, a bibliography of primary and secondary works and an index. Issues of racial, national and cultural identity are explored, as are gender and sexuality. Books in the series also examine writers' use of genre, particularly ways in which Western genres are adapted or subverted and 'traditional' local forms are reworked in a contemporary context.

Contemporary World Writers aims to bring together the theoretical impulse which currently dominates post-colonial studies and closely argued readings of particular authors' works, and by so doing to avoid the danger of appropriating the specifics of particular texts into the hegemony of totalising theories.

List of abbreviations

Chronology

1947   Salman Rushdie born in Bombay, in the year of Indian independence from British rule, to Muslim businessman Anis Ahmed Rushdie and his wife Negin.

1954   Begins attending an English mission school in Bombay.

1961   Aged 14, sent to study at Rugby School in England.

1964   Family moves to Karachi in Pakistan.

1965–8 Attends Kings College, Cambridge where he reads History and acts in the Footlights Revue.

1968–9 Continues acting at the Oval House, Kennington, in London.

1969   Meets Clarissa Luard. Gives up acting to work as an advertising copywriter for a year. Stops work to write an unpublished novel, *The Book of The Pir*. Takes up copywriting again, working on a part-time basis which allows him to continue writing.

1975   *Grimus* published by Victor Gollancz. Begins work on *Midnight's Children*.

1976   Marries Clarissa Luard.

1981   Leaves advertising in the spring prior to the publication of *Midnight's Children* by Jonathan Cape. Wins the Booker and James Tait Black prizes and an English Speaking Union Literary Award.

1983   *Shame* published by Jonathan Cape. Shortlisted for the Booker Prize, and wins France's Prix du Meilleur Livre Étranger. Begins work on *The Satanic Verses*.

1984   Travels through Central Australia with the writer Bruce Chatwin.

1986   Visits Nicaragua as a guest of the Sandinista Association of
Cultural Workers.

1987   Jonathan Cape publishes the travelogue resulting from his
Nicaragua trip – *The Jaguar Smile: A Nicaraguan Journey*.
Book is dedicated to the Australian travel writer, Robyn
Davidson, with whom he had become involved. Marriage to
Clarissa Luard is dissolved.

1988   Marries American novelist Marianne Wiggins. *The Satanic
Verses* published by Viking/Penguin. Shortlisted for the
Booker Prize and wins the Whitbread Prize for Best Novel.
Book banned in India and South Africa.

1989   *The Satanic Verses* burnt publicly in Bradford, England.
Iran's religious leader, Ayatollah Khomeini, pronounces
fatwa on Rushdie, condemning him to death for blasphemy.
There is a £1.5 million bounty placed on his head. Rushdie
and Wiggins go into hiding under police protection. Wiggins
separates from him.

1990   *Haroun and the Sea of Stories* published by Granta. Wins a
Writer's Guild award.

1991   *Imaginary Homelands*, a collection of reviews, essays and
criticism over ten years, published by Granta.

1992   *The Wizard of Oz* published as part of the British Film Institute's Film Classics series. Marriage to Marianne Wiggins is
dissolved.

1994   *East, West*, a collection of short stories, the majority of
which had previously appeared in print, is published by
Jonathan Cape.

1995   Rushdie's latest major work, *The Moor's Last Sigh*, published by Jonathan Cape. The fatwa has not been rescinded
and Rushdie remains in hiding.

Contexts and intertexts

IN *The Satanic Verses*, the narrative voice poses the question – 'How does newness come into the world?'[1] The answer is an affirmation of the process by which Rushdie's art and indeed his identity as a writer has been produced. Newness is 'melange, hotch-potch, a bit of this and a bit of that'.[2] Any attempt to explain the features and preoccupations of Rushdie's fiction must take account of the diverse cultural elements that combine to give his work its characteristic style.

Rushdie's early life as the only son of a professional, middle-class Muslim family in Bombay must be seen as a crucial factor in any assessment of his subsequent literary output. The family spoke the Muslim language of Urdu, but Rushdie learnt English from the age of five in English-medium schools[3] and was encouraged by his parents to use English at home as the language of everyday discourse. The dual consciousness, created as a result of this linguistic division, is the source of much of the versatility and play in Rushdie's use of English in his fiction. Aside from the ambiguities and complexities of his use of English, which will be returned to later, Rushdie also sees his own light skin as of significance in the way his identity is perceived by others. Despite attempts to end ingrained discrimination in Indian society resulting from the caste system, a light skin is still a measure of beauty and an attribute much sought after, particularly in a bride. Rushdie's own comparatively fair complexion, in combination with his privileged education at the heart of the British establishment and his perfect, accentless English have marked him out as simultaneously 'other' but recognisably 'the same'. It is as if Rushdie embodies in his own person the hybridity which for the cultural theorist Homi K. Bhabha 'terrorizes authority with the ruse of recognition, its mimicry, its mockery'.[4] Despite Rushdie's antipathy to the work of the novelist Paul Scott, expressed in his essay 'Outside the Whale' (IH, 89–90), it is tempting to see in his own identity a reflection of Scott's creation, Hari Kumar, from *The Raj Quartet* – the English-educated Indian gentleman, too Indian for the English and too English for the Indians, rootless and disaffiliated like the outcast Philoctetes whose name he adopts.

Saladin Chamcha's discomfiture in the English public school to which he is sent in *The Satanic Verses* mirrors Rushdie's own feelings of alienation at Rugby,[5] while the voice and presence of both writer and creation appear almost parodic of the persona of the 'English gentleman', exhibiting what Bhabha has called 'the indeterminacy of diasporic identity' and 'the irresolvable, borderline culture of hybridity'.[6] Yet Rushdie, like Bhabha and other theorists of cultural identity, abjures the apparent confusion and 'homelessness' implicit in such a characterisation in favour of the idea of hybridity as a positive category. In place of the negative connotations of displacement and dislocation which would seem to be the inevitable result of his removal from Bombay and his family, Rushdie asks us in both *Shame* and his non-fictional writing to accept that he has gained as well as lost something 'in translation'.[7] Beyond the individual, the assertion that new, plural and eclectic identities are now the norm rather than the exception is also offered as a way out of the racisms and xenophobic nationalisms which bedevil contemporary society.

An important incident in Rushdie's youth which irrevocably altered the pattern of his own life was his loss of faith in the family religion of Islam. This loss, and the resulting god-shaped hole in his own identity, is the source of much of the religious debate in his novels and essays and, arguably, lies at the root of the situation in which he currently finds himself. Rushdie's responses to religion in general and Islam in particular are more complex than they might at first appear. For example, the reliance on aspects of Hindu mythology, particularly in *Midnight's Children*, may appear odd for a writer of Muslim origin. One answer to this lies in the polyglot nature of Indian society with its blend of Hinduism, Islam, Buddhism, Christianity and many other religious communities.

Two aspects of India's majority Hindu culture in particular coalesce in informing Rushdie's work – the influence of Hindu mythical archetypes which still permeates Indian society and the brash, commercial promulgation of these myths through the hugely popular Indian film industry: the 'Bombay talkies'. As Anuradha Dingwaney Needham says of *Midnight's Children*, Saleem's narrative is 'crucially dependent on an acute insider's familiarity with that most ubiquitous icon of the subcontinent's popular culture – Bombay cinema'.[8] Religion, politics and myth form a seamless whole in Indian culture as a text like *The Satanic Verses* seeks to demonstrate. Gibreel Farishta earns his living playing avatars of the Hindu pantheon in films, before becoming a figurehead for the politicisation of contemporary British Asian youth. The wealth and availability of mythical constructs make them almost inevitable intertexts of Rushdie's work.

It is perhaps difficult for a western reader to comprehend the continuing degree of interplay between contemporary Indian culture and its mythical parallel. Rushdie's fiction is no exception in the way it interweaves contemporary and mythical 'realities', benefiting from what the writer himself has termed the 'cultural accumulation' of myth.[9] His characters commandeer the identities of mythic figures, such as are found in the pages of the Indian epic narratives the *Mahabharata* and *Ramayana*. This can take the form of an explicit borrowing as in the representation of Shiva and Parvati in *Midnight's Children*, or a more subtle manifestation as in Rushdie's collection of short stories, *East, West*. Here, in 'The Courter', the hall porter Mecir (or Mixed-Up) takes his Indian friend, the retired ayah Mary, on the London Underground where her sari gets caught in an escalator.

> She was forced to spin round and round like a top... It was
> Mixed-Up who saved her by pushing the emergency stop

> button before the sari was completely unwound and she
> was exposed in her petticoat for all the world to see.[10]

The scene is a contemporary replaying of the attempted stripping of Draupadi, wife of the Pandava brothers, by Duhsasana in the epic the *Mahabharata*.

> In vain Duhsasana toiled to strip off her garments, for, as
> he pulled off each, ever fresh garments were seen to clothe
> her body, and soon a great heap of resplendent clothes was
> piled up before the assembly till Duhsasana desisted.[11]

As the following chapters hope to illustrate, the gradually increasing references to Islam in Rushdie's work are indicative of the exploratory nature of his fiction, leading him and his readers on a journey of discovery through different aspects of his personal, cultural and national identity. As such, Islam had to be reckoned with eventually in his writing. Despite his open hostility to what he sees as the darker byproducts of religious fundamentalism, Rushdie's work is nevertheless suffused not only with borrowings from and reworkings of Hindu myths, but also with elements of, for example, Sufism, the mystical wing of Islam, which appeals to him intellectually if not spiritually. Indeed, Sara Suleri has commented that, despite the uproar over its alleged blasphemies, *The Satanic Verses* is in fact 'a deeply Islamic book'[12] while Timothy Brennan in *Salman Rushdie and the Third World* sees the *Qur'ān* itself as an important intertext of *Shame*.[13] It is certainly true that the importance accorded religion in Rushdie's fiction is evidence of the lasting effects of his Indian/Muslim background rather than the more recent influences of western secularism on the formation of his identity. Similarly the rejection of faith both by Rushdie himself and by a number of his characters can never be viewed as an unequivocally affirmative event. Both experience the need to fill the god-shaped hole with other compensatory factors, whether literature or women.[14]

The intertextuality of Rushdie's fiction with film is another area where east meets west in his work, for if the Bombay talkies with their flamboyant over-the-top quality have influenced his technique, so too have exemplars of the European avant-garde. Godard, Truffaut, Buñuel – all are cited by Rushdie as sources of the surrealist tendencies in his fiction.[15] This intertextuality is more than a matter of paying homage to the film greats with deliberate echoes of their work. It extends to the adoption and translation of a filmic vocabulary into literary texts. These effects are perhaps most in evidence in *Midnight's Children* and *The Satanic Verses*, but as the chapter on *Haroun* argues, Rushdie is also keen to suggest a cartoon-like quality in the visual aspects of his prose. The transference of film terminology to text is a feature of the work of contemporary postmodernist writers such as Angela Carter,[16] where 'freeze frames' and 'rewinds' allow for the manipulation of textual time and the opportunity of commenting on the nature and importance of memory.

The extent to which Rushdie would embrace the label of 'postmodern' writer for himself is debatable and will be considered more fully in the critical overview at the end of this study. Whatever conclusion is reached by the individual reader, it is clear that Rushdie's work blends a wide-ranging knowledge of Eastern literature, culture and history (he studied history rather than literature at university) with a correspondingly broad appreciation of their Western counterparts, combining them in a technically erudite and theoretically aware whole.

As this statement implies, Rushdie's literary precursors are manifold and his allusiveness almost exhausting in its density. He has enumerated in various interviews, particularly in the early 1980s, the western literary sources from which he believes his work springs. Direct allusion to or structural parallels with medieval artists such as Dante and Boccaccio, eastern European masters such as Gogol, Kafka and Bulgakov, and experimental modernists such as Joyce and Brecht are commonplace. More contemporary influences are European and Latin American 'magical realists' such as Calvino, Borges and Gabriel García Márquez.[17]

In contrast, beyond invoking the somewhat enigmatic figure of the 'storyteller of Baroda' in a 1983 lecture-cum-interview,[18] Rushdie had not, until recently, insisted on a correspondingly explicit roll-call of Eastern influences on his work. As already mentioned, the Sanskrit epics of the *Mahabharata* and *Ramayana* are clearly influential, while other compendia of stories such as the *Katha-Sarit-Sagar*[19] and the *Arabian Nights* or *The One Thousand and One Nights*[20] are explicit or implicit intertexts of his work. The *Qur'ān*, in its incarnation as art rather than the word of God, is clearly important, as are other Eastern intertexts such as Sufi and Urdu poetry. Rushdie tended to dissociate himself from the early Indo-Anglian[21] writers such as Raja Rao and Mulk Raj Anand but has increasingly come to share their views on the 'decolonization' of the English language by former subject peoples, and on the importance of the political aspect of literature.

To understand the significance of Rushdie's handling of language, it is first necessary to appreciate the arguments made both by himself and other Indian writers in favour of the idea of Indian-English or English used in a specifically and recognisably Indian way. In his essay '"Commonwealth Literature" Does Not Exist', Rushdie states that 'the English language ceased to be the sole possession of the English some time ago'. (*IH*, 70) For a writer in Rushdie's position, who cannot escape the legacy of his education, employment of English is less contentious than it would have been for pre-independence Indian writers, whose work needed to operate on one level as a contestation of colonial authority in itself.

Raja Rao, in the foreword to his 1938 novel *Kanthapura*, described English as a language that was simultaneously alien and familiar.[22] For him, the split manifested itself between the areas of intellectual and emotional life. Forced to recognise and accept the dominance of the coloniser's language, to then attempt to deny its influence – its permeation of the Indian psyche – would be to pretend that the Indian writer occupies a different socio-cultural situation than is in fact the case.

Rushdie's attitude, understandably more positive in some respects than Rao's, is that the use of English by any writer from a formerly colonised nation is an assertion of identity rather than an indication of its loss. In his essay 'Imaginary Homelands' he writes:

> Those of us who do use English do so in spite of our ambiguity towards it, or perhaps because of that, perhaps because we can find in that linguistic struggle a reflection of other struggles… To conquer English may be to complete the process of making ourselves free. (*IH*, 17)

But of course, the Indian writer does not defeat the colonial legacy of English by mere assertion. Mulk Raj Anand, another of the first major Indian writers to work in English, attempted an analysis of the process by which English is Indianised in his essay 'Pigeon Indian: Some Notes on Indian-English Writing.'[23] Having accepted the centrality of English as a medium for Indian writers to employ, Anand attempts to distinguish some of the characteristics of such usage. He differentiates between its uses in spoken and imaginative contexts. His term 'pigeon Indian' is coined to denote the imaginative employment of Indian-English in literature. An important feature of 'pigeon Indian', which is also borne out by Rushdie's writing, is its complex and symbiotic relationship with the writer's Indian mother tongue:

> even when Indians know English grammar, and have been used to speaking the alien tongue for a long time, they tend to feel and think in their own mother tongues. Often, the native speech enters into the shell of the sentence in the foreign language.[24]

This process is also reciprocal for the coloniser, as Anand points out by referring to the large number of Indian words which have filtered into everyday English usage.

Rushdie is also forced to admit the flexibility of English,[25] a flexibility which allows him to convey both the rhythm and sense of the many different Indian dialects without needing to employ any or all of them. This is the source of such phrases in his work as 'donkey-from-somewhere', a direct translation of a Hindi expression,[26] and of Naseem Aziz's repetition of 'whatsitsname' in *Midnight's Children*.[27] The rhythm of the language is, of course, partly a product of the influence of the Indian epics and of Indian oral storytelling, which will be examined more closely in the section on *Midnight's Children*. 'We tell one interminable tale,', writes Rao. 'Episode follows episode, and when our thoughts stop our breath stops, and we move on to another thought. This was and still is the ordinary style of our storytelling.'[28]

To return to the question of the Indian literary precursors of Rushdie's style, we are confronted with the problem of unravelling the claims for a recognisable cultural continuity from the reality of writers' individualised techniques and agendas. In a 1982 newspaper article, 'The Empire Writes Back with a Vengeance',[29] Rushdie wrote of the influence of the Indian writer and philosopher G. V. Desani on his work. Desani's 1948 novel, *All About H. Hatterr*, is the 'autobiographical' of an Indian and his encounter with the seven sages of India. It is a comic novel, but one whose comedy has a peculiar edge to it as a result of the linguistically taxing nature of the text. Do we laugh at Hatterr or at English as we experience the absurdities of the language when forced through Desani's hoops? The disruption of English is the classic gesture of defiance towards western cultural imperialism on the part of the post-colonial writer.

Desani's novel certainly seems to offer itself as a model from which later writers could draw lessons in the construction of the linguistically hybrid novel, though Rushdie tries to take this process of hybridisation a stage further by imbuing every aspect of his novels with a sense of their own and his own confused 'parentage'. 'I write rigmarole English,' declares Hatterr, 'straining your goodly godly tongue'.[30] Desani's own background – born in Nairobi and subsequently residing in both Britain and the United States – presents another common factor with Rushdie through his migrancy. Similarly the links between *All About H. Hatterr* and, for example, *Midnight's Children*, are clear. Published in the year following Indian independence, Desani's novel is a world away from the ponderous, overtly politicised work of Rao and Anand. Its tone is one of exhilaration, if not in new-found freedom itself, then in the liberation of language and expression that seem to have resulted from it. Its quality of orality leads one to imagine that it would work well – if not better – as a monologue on radio. The tone is exclamatory, breathless, and its habit of running together groups of nouns and adjectives for emphasis is a clear link with a later characteristic of Rushdie's prose:

> There was no transparent amber and cider sunshine-glow, which I had accustomed myself into imagining as a perpetual God's gift aura over England, from stolen peeps into Rev. the Head's privately-owned Our Lovely Homeland type of sunny Devon-Cornwall illustrated-in-tricolour publication... No: instead by Pitt ('88) and Gladstone ('86)! lightning, clang o'doom, thunder, and Glasgow fury![31]

Rushdie's style in *Midnight's Children* is thus in one respect a smoothing out of the disjointed tone of Hatterr's narrative. Part of the effect of stringing unpunctuated words together is to give the narrative greater fluidity. The style of Hatterr's speech – often discarding pronouns and other extraneous matter – is a curious mixture of the clipped, militaristic speech of India's former rulers (the staple of any 'club' conversation in a Raj novel) and the naturally disjointed utterances of anyone unfamiliar with the syntax and grammar of a language, who has picked up phrases, catchwords, expressions and exclamations which are then pieced together to give the impression of familiarity with the language. In this sense, the language of Desani's novel can be said to correspond to the wider impression gained of India itself in *Midnight's Children*, with its blend of English and Indian, epic art and Bombay talkie, political rhetoric and street-traders' lingo. The result is inevitably hybrid. Rushdie makes the claim that *All About H. Hatterr*:

> showed how English could be bent and kneaded until it spoke in an authentically Indian voice... Desani's triumph was to take Babu-English... and turn it against itself: the instrument of subservience became a weapon of liberation. It was the first great stroke of the decolonizing pen.[32]

This image of the 'decolonizing pen' indicates Rushdie's belief that writing 'in a language that is not one's own'[33] and seeking to represent life beyond colonialism is an inherently political act. M. D. Fletcher, in his introduction to *Reading Rushdie*, suggests in effect that the 'politics' of Rushdie's writing, in the broadest sense of the word, are the most significant aspect of his work.[34] As far as defining Rushdie's personal politics is concerned, his plight in recent years has forced him to occupy a sometimes ambiguous position between espousals of individualist and collectivist ideologies. In the wake of *Shame*'s publication, Rushdie described his politics as 'broadly speaking Marxist'.[35] He went on to speak of his own view of the alternative to the politics of Indira Gandhi in India:

> I would have thought that Marxist politics have much more relevance in India than they have in some Western countries. Some of the Marxist rhetoric which now sounds very passé and dated when you apply it to Western countries still means very important things when you apply it to those countries. So I suppose if you want a simple answer to the solution, I would propose it in largely Marxist terms.[36]

The vagueness of his actual position at this time is perhaps implicit in the terms of its declaration – a 'broadly', 'largely' Marxist position may just mean liberalism that is radical as well as woolly. Richard Cronin in *Imagining India* believes this to be so:

> In place of Kipling's imperialism Salman Rushdie offers his own, somewhat vague liberal prejudices which he sometimes – mistakenly – imagines to be consistent with Marxism. It is the defining characteristic of this kind of liberalism that it cannot reconcile its values with any political machinery that would enforce them.[37]

The debates thrown up by Rushdie's present circumstances surrounding the concept of a writer's freedom of expression, highlight the difficult, even impossible, political position which Rushdie seems to occupy. Any radical left-wing politics are muddied as he becomes increasingly drawn towards John Stuart Mill's individualist conception of liberty rather than Engels's view of freedom as the consciousness of necessity. One need not doubt the sincerity of Rushdie's desire for an egalitarian, socialist solution to society's problems world-wide to argue that he cannot be regarded seriously as a philosophical Marxist.

One of the many painful results of his current isolation has been his loss of status as a spokesman for British Asians. He had previously been involved in anti-racist campaigns and endorsed projects designed to affirm the image of Britain as a multicultural society.[38] The public burning of *The Satanic Verses* in the streets of Bradford and the widespread outrage at his alleged blasphemies against Islam have, perhaps irredeemably, sullied that record. He has tried to replace that loss in part, and even perhaps to recapture the heady idealism of his days with the rebel Sandinistas in Nicaragua, by speaking out on issues of wider international concern such as the current crisis in former Yugoslavia.[39] The arrogance of the creative artist, which is arguably necessary, and the sincere political beliefs of the individual man often appear in conflict and at best reside in uneasy compromise with each other.

Where then does one begin in drawing together the elements that constitute the work of such an allusive, elusive, erudite, arrogant, political and theoretically informed writer? Endings may tend to precede beginnings in Rushdie's own fictions,[40] but this study will attempt to adopt a more prosaic pattern of development and begin at the beginning.

Grimus

Rushdie's first novel, *Grimus*, offers an important insight into stylistic and thematic preoccupations developed more fully in the author's later work. The models for *Grimus* within both Eastern and Western traditions are diverse – Dante's *Divine Comedy*, Farid ud-Din 'Attar's *Conference of the Birds* (*Mantiq al-Tayr*), even Samuel Johnson's *Rasselas*, with the hero Flapping Eagle and his sister choosing to escape the particular social restrictions and conformities of their own less-than-Happy Valley. At this stage in Rushdie's development, the diversity remains just that; the elements insufficiently blended to make the novel appear a skilfully amalgamated whole.

The novel was written with the Victor Gollancz Science Fiction Prize in mind,[1] though, as will be discussed later, it fails to occupy a comfortable place within the genre. Its indebtedness to other literary forms exceeds the cleverly allusive to overstretch itself in often tedious mimicry of other writers. With its adolescent conceits and punning,[2] its loss of narrative control and its uninvolving characters, it is very much a test-run for the successful novels of the 1980s.

Viewed from the standpoint of *The Satanic Verses*, *Grimus* allows us to see areas of debate which are subsequently handled with greater depth and maturity in Rushdie's later work – ideas of personal and national identity, the legacy of colonialism, the problems of exile and even the first signs of a tendency to demonise female sexuality. A crucial aspect of these discussions in Rushdie's later novels is his use of a specific geographical setting, not only to evoke a particular atmosphere but, through its cultural and historical associations, to raise certain issues for the reader. For Timothy Brennan in *Salman Rushdie and the Third World*, *Grimus*'s lack of a specific and identifiable geographical location is its chief failure:

> It would be hard to find a novel that demonstrated better the truth of Fanon's claim that a culture that is not national is meaningless... they must be anchored in a coherent 'structure of feeling', which only actual communities can create.[3]

The need for a post-colonial national culture, discussed by the psychiatrist and theorist of colonisation Frantz Fanon in *The Wretched of the Earth*, highlights Rushdie's own problem, in *Grimus* and beyond it, of producing a new kind of literature; a new kind of cultural representation that is an amalgam of both the Eastern and Western influences that comprise his experience. The 'native intellectual' experiences the desire 'to shrink away from that Western culture in which they all risk being swamped'[4] says Fanon, but then encounters the obstacle whereby the 'national culture' to which s/he turns 'can hardly supply any figureheads which will bear comparison with those, so many in number, and so great in prestige, of the occupying power's civilisation'.[5] This is, in a sense, the 'problem' of *Grimus* – its desire to incorporate a variety of literary styles and products into a framework which, as Brennan puts it, '"tries on" cultures like used clothing'.[6]

In so far as *Grimus* is located anywhere, its depiction of the Amerindian culture of the Axona makes tentative first steps towards an examination of post-coloniality. As with the inhabitants of Johnson's Happy Valley, 'no Axona had ever descended from this plateau to the plains beneath'.[7] The voyage out is both an exploration of alternative societies and a confrontation with the forces of change, here linked to the image of an oppressive white power. Phoenix, Flapping Eagle's first port of call, combines the material trappings of progress with the soulless conformity of Western capitalism – 'automobiles and launderettes and juke boxes and all kinds of machines and people dressed in dusty clothes with a kind of despair in their eyes'. (*G*, 21) The Axona, for all their own prejudices, possess customs and a social framework that offer a sense of community and identity which the people of Phoenix lack.

The link with *Rasselas* may also hint at the concern with post-coloniality that is the undeveloped side of *Grimus*. Johnson's full title, *The History of Rasselas, Prince of Abyssinia*, provides a link to a minor and somewhat feeble comic motif in *Grimus*. The mysterious Nicholas Deggle, expelled from the town of K for his attempted destruction of the source of Grimus's power, first encounters Flapping Eagle in Phoenix and, eventually and unwittingly, leads him towards his final confrontation with Grimus:

> [Deggle] came and went his unknowable way, sauntering in and out of Mrs Cramm's villa on the southern coast of Morispain, and every time he left, he would wave un-smilingly and say:- Ethiopia! It was a complex and awful joke, arising from the archaic name of that closed, hidden, historical country (Abyssinia... I'll be seeing you) and it drove Flapping Eagle out of his mind every time it was said. (*G*, 28)

This mention of Rasselas's kingdom may indicate just how submerged the question of post-coloniality is in the novel. As the only African country never to be colonised, Abyssinia/Ethiopia continues to hold a particular significance for all those whose identities are a product of colonialism.

The links to Johnson's tale of utopian disaffection are reinforced when Flapping Eagle drinks the elixir of life brought to him from Grimus by his sister Bird-Dog. His centuries-long sea journey illustrates the burden of perpetual existence for Flapping Eagle. The problems of longevity are equally oppressive to Rasselas: 'He had been before terrified at the length of life which nature promised him, because he considered that in a long time much must be endured.'[8]

What will become a familiar preoccupation in Rushdie's work with protagonists of confused or mysterious parentage is first revealed in Flapping Eagle's characterisation, alongside the whiteness of his skin that sets apart the hero, like Rushdie himself, from the majority of his compatriots. In his various guises of

Born-from-Dead, Joe-Sue and Flapping Eagle, Rushdie's hero prefigures the divided identities of Gibreel and Saladin in *The Satanic Verses*. As the demonised Saladin is informed, it is the fate of the migrant post-colonial subject to be 'invented' by his oppressors, and to succumb to the requirements of that character invention. The mutations of Flapping Eagle's identity demonstrate an awareness of the cultural and political implications of names. Just as Saladin Chamcha re-embraces India through the identity of Salahuddin Chamchawala, so Flapping Eagle is granted true Amerindian status by the eagle that names him, leaving behind the stigmata of androgyny and posthumous birth.

Flapping Eagle's voyage away from Phoenix elicits a passage of illuminating if rather self-indulgent prose. The deployment of a multiplicity of narrative voices in his work is one of Rushdie's most notable achievements. It is an idea he is clearly grappling with notionally in this passage. Flapping Eagle encounters a T. S. Eliot-like figure on his travels:

> A man rehearsing voices on a cliff-top: high whining voices, low gravelly voices, subtle insinuating voices, voices honeyed with pain, voices glinting with laughter, the voices of the birds and of the fishes. He asked the man what he was doing (as he sailed by). The man called back – and each word was the word of a different being:- I am looking for a suitable voice to speak in. (*G*, 32)

It is not so much that *The Satanic Verses* speaks in one voice, but that Rushdie's 'ear' for dialogue, and the ease with which he moves between cultures and historical periods, is more sophisticated in the latter work. This passage shows an alternative narrative voice breaking out, but the skilful manipulation of polyphony and the endless readings this can produce is debated here rather then embarked on.

Alongside the reference to polyphony goes a description of Flapping Eagle's chameleon nature, constantly adapting to the changes in his environment and others' attitudes towards him:

> Stripped of his past, forsaking the language of his ancestors for the language of the archipelagos of the world, forsaking

the ways of his ancestors for those of the places he drifted
to... he lived, doing what he was given to do, thinking what
he was instructed to think, being what it was most desir-
able to be... and doing it so skilfully... that the men he
encountered thought he was thus of his own free will and
liked him for it. (G, 32)

This is surely an attempt at assessing the condition of the migrant
post-colonial subject that stops short of the direct and personal-
ised accounts that we find in *Shame* and *The Satanic Verses*. The
prose touches on the acquiescence of the native subject in his own
reinvention, but fails to push its argument home. Flapping Eagle
is at one and the same time the hero of a nascent and tentative
study of migrant identity, and of a chaotic fantasy with no immediately discernible arguments of any import. The voyage of
discovery buckles under the weight of the different elements it
seeks to assimilate.

Where *Grimus*'s links with *Rasselas* are largely thematic,
Rushdie's borrowings from Dante consist of topographical and
stylistic devices. His most obvious debt to Dante is the use of
Virgil Jones as Flapping Eagle's guide. As the poet Virgil leads
Dante through Hell and Purgatory to a vision of God in Paradise,
so Virgil Jones leads Flapping Eagle in his ascent of Calf Mountain towards Grimus.

In the introduction to her translation of the *Divine Comedy*,
Dorothy L. Sayers notes that, in popular tradition, Virgil was
often regarded as a white magician. In this vein, Virgil Jones is
able to master many of the supernatural obstacles on the path to
Grimus and protect his charge. When the poet Virgil assumes his
role as Dante's guide in Canto I of *Hell*, he indicates that a wor-
thier soul than he will actually lead Dante to his culminating
vision of Paradise. This figure is Beatrice. For Flapping Eagle,
Virgil Jones's place is taken by the far-from-beatific Media, a
whore from Madame Jocasta's brothel in K.

The topography of both Dante's Hell and Rushdie's Calf
Mountain is such that their navigation entails journeys within
journeys. The routes up Mount Purgatory and Calf Mountain
require travellers to negotiate other dimensions existing simul-

taneously with the overriding geographical features in the narratives. Cantos V to VIII of *Hell* correspond almost exactly to the movements of Flapping Eagle and Virgil Jones in two chapters of *Grimus*. In the latter, the travellers enter the Inner Dimension of Calf Mountain. They must negotiate a series of concentric circles in order to be brought back into a waking state. They journey on bicycles through a tunnel which takes them to a river bank. In the distance is a lake with a tall, stone circular building at the centre. Flapping Eagle passes across to the tower in a boat and, after his encounter with the goddess Axona, is brought back to consciousness.

In the *Divine Comedy*, Dante and Virgil begin their descent through the circles of Hell in Canto V. They find Hell-Gate in the wilderness of Mount Purgatory and cross the River Acheron on the edge of Upper Hell. In Canto VII they spy the watchtower by the marsh of Styx and in Canto VIII a boat is dispatched to fetch the two men to the tower. Just as Calf Mountain both rests on and effectively *is* Calf Island, so Mount Purgatory, as Sayers informs us, is a lofty mountain rising out of the sea in the Antipodes.[9] Both are banked by sandy shores and both Dante and Flapping Eagle have to negotiate forests and bad weather on their ascents. The final, less directly transferred correspondence between the two texts is the use of a symbolic rose in both narratives. The Stone Rose is the source of Grimus's power which must be broken to destroy his continuing control over the mountain and the people of K. The Celestial Rose in Dante's *Paradise* is a symbol of divine love – rather than the authority of a mystical deity – and depicts the saints in Heaven on each of its white petals.

Grimus does not restrict its intertexts to Western literary models. The most direct Eastern influence upon its construction is the *Conference of the Birds* (*Mantiq al-Tayr*), a twelfth-century religious poem by the Sufi mystic Farid ud-Din 'Attar. Despite Rushdie's declaration in a 1984 interview that his interest in Sufism had diminished,[10] it is to some of the figures within 'Attar's narrative that he returns in *Haroun and the Sea of Stories*. It is possible to speculate on the comfort offered by such a model to a writer as beleaguered as Rushdie was when writing

Haroun. Despite its more sophisticated handling, there was something of a return to the earlier 'innocence' of *Grimus* in the move. The return to Sufi symbolism may mark an attempt to reconcile the fundamental conflict between the expression of unity that is the basis of Islam – 'There is no god but God' – and Rushdie's own movement towards, and increasing embrace of, multiplicity: cultural, social, linguistic and spiritual. The professed project of a union between Islamic culture and the demands of post-colonial postmodernity (for those who do not believe or care that it was achieved in *The Satanic Verses*) will perhaps require the influence of Sufism to reassert itself in his writing.

The *Conference* depicts the search of the bird 'kingdom' for a ruler. That ruler is the Simurg (of which Grimus is an anagram) who dwells on Kaf (Calf) Mountain. The birds are led by the Hoopoe (who also figures in *Haroun*), who is singled out by his markings as particularly favoured. He examines the birds to see who is willing and able to undertake the journey to the Simurg. The Hoopoe sets out the difficulties of the journey ahead in a way that similarly describes the mysterious power of Grimus:

> We have a true king, he lives behind the mountain called
> Kaf. His name is Simurgh and he is the king of the birds.
> He is close to us but we are far from him. The place where
> he dwells is inaccessible, and no tongue is able to utter his
> name... He is the sovran lord and is bathed in the perfec-
> tion of his majesty. He does not manifest himself com-
> pletely even in the place of his dwelling, and to this no
> knowledge or intelligence can attain.[11]

As with *Rasselas*, there is a link to ideas of longevity and immortality. The poem mentions the water of life drunk by Al-Khizr in the time of Abraham which conferred the gift of immortality on him.

The notion of the quest is central to Sufism. It is the means by which the adherent moves towards the divine centre, where the multiplicity of existence is seen to be gathered into totality and unity. The birds in the *Conference* thus discover that their ultimate goal is realisation of their unity with the Simurg. Only thirty of them survive the quest – Simurg itself means 'thirty birds' – and are taken up into a unity of being with their creator:

'they did not know if they were still themselves or if they had become the Simurgh. At last, in a state of contemplation, they realized that they were the Simurgh and that the Simurgh was the thirty birds.'[12]

The cosmic mountain of Kaf/Qaf in Sufism has a significance beyond the merely topographical detail it provides in *Grimus*. That mountain-climbing for Rushdie, Dante and 'Attar possesses some symbolic significance is evident, but it varies between the texts. For Rushdie, it would seem no more than a stylistic device that an arduous ascent is called for from Flapping Eagle in order to achieve his desired goal, though reunion with his sister Bird-Dog seems somewhat lame as a directing force for such a generally aimless character. Timothy Brennan sees it as a representation of the social climbing of the emigrant[13] but such a meaning is too deeply buried in the text to validate this argument. Its spiritual rather than social symbolism is far greater. For the Sufi:

> mountain climbing corresponds to the inner aspects of life… One needs a guide to climb: one can climb a mountain by many paths, but one needs to follow one made by experienced people… one passes the tree-line and enters the world with-out forms. One passes from form to formlessness, from sensible to intelligible. The name of the person who reaches the top of the cosmic mountain is Simurgh.[14]

The topography is repeated in *Grimus*: there is a point at the edge of the Forest of Calf where the travellers enter alternative states. The Sufi quest entails a passage through four Gardens of Paradise: the gardens of the Soul, Heart, Spirit and Essence. The Fountain of Life or Immortality is encountered in the Garden of the Heart, while the Garden of Essence requires of the Sufi-to-be a surrender of individual identity. Brennan sees the goal of the quest in *Grimus* as 'a transcendent vision of heterogeneity'.[15] This in some ways is the central quest of Rushdie's writing – the assimilation of cultural diversity within artistic unity. Rushdie arguably loses – or at least fails to establish – his own authorial identity in *Grimus*. The succesful assertion of heterogeneity and hybridity comes much later.

Rushdie's failure to engage fully with questions of migrant identity in *Grimus* has led to a dissipation of critical interest, away from the seeds of the engagement and towards more abstruse theorisation of the novel's complex structure. A rare assessment of the novel, Ib Johansen's essay 'The Flight from the Enchanter: Reflections on Salman Rushdie's *Grimus*',[16] acknowledges a Prospero/Caliban relationship between Flapping Eagle and Grimus, but fails to explore the novel's (admittedly flimsy) treatment of post-coloniality. Johansen likens *Grimus* to the forms of Menippean satire as defined by Mikhail Bakhtin. Examination of *Problems of Dostoevsky's Poetics* highlights Rushdie's employment of elements of the genre in his construction of *Grimus*. According to Bakhtin, Menippean satire:

> is characterized by an extraordinary freedom of plot and philosophical invention... [while its] bold and unrestrained use of the fantastic and adventure is internally motivated, justified by and devoted to a purely ideational and philosophical end: the creation of extraordinary situations for the provoking and testing of a philosophical idea, a discourse, a truth, embodied in the image of a wise man, the seeker of this truth.[17]

Brothels and taverns, we are told, such as Madame Jocasta's and the Elbaroom in *Grimus*, are the kind of place where the adventures of Menippean satire occur. The confusion of genres and philosophies in *Grimus* means that the truth sought by Flapping Eagle is never clear, never entirely spiritual in a Sufi sense, nor entirely secular, as the book's modernist tendencies might seem to demand. The undeclared quest for the explication and re-integration of the post-colonial identity is side-stepped, and the goal of the journey dissolves in the final moments of the novel's apocalyptic denouement.

At this stage of Rushdie's writing, the text offers little more than a mirror of the techniques and conventions of Menippean satire as Bakhtin sees them. But there is within Bakhtin's study an interesting precursor to the treatment of multiple realities and divided identities in Rushdie's later work:

> Dreams, daydreams, insanity destroy the epic and tragic
> wholeness of a person and his fate: the possibilities of an-
> other person and another life are revealed in him, he loses
> his finalized quality and ceases to mean only one thing; he
> ceases to coincide with himself.[18]

Grimus can only register that disjunction and multiplicity through
a jarring blend of fantastic episodes and philosophies. *The Satanic
Verses*, with its integral use of dream sequences and its implicit
and explicit concern with 'cultural schizophrenia', is the exemplification of Bakhtin's idea within the context of post-colonial writing.

The notion of Flapping Eagle's 'difference' is established
without recourse to any examination of the 'othering' of the
post-colonial subject. Flapping Eagle is too white for the Axona
and different from them by the manner of his birth. But there is
nothing about him to suggest any fundamental difference from
the figures of oppression that appear in the novel. He is no
Saladin Chamcha, the ubiquitous 'Paki' confronting the prejudices and bigotry of 'Proper London'. The idea of exile within the
novel subsequently retains a Joycean rather than migrant aspect:
the misunderstood young man, forced to leave home on a literal
and figurative voyage of discovery. There are, however, glimpses
of the greater understanding of exile as intimately connected to
the condition of post-coloniality. Flapping Eagle, newly arrived
in K, sees through a window an old woman examining her past in
the form of a photograph album. 'It is the natural condition of
the exile – putting down roots in memories.'(*G*, 107) In this context, the statement is almost a *non sequitur*. The link between
the old woman's nostalgia and the concept of exile is a tenuous
one. It is as if the important concerns and messages of Rushdie's
writing as a whole are attempting to surface through the confusions of this bizarre narrative. Later, Virgil Jones's ex-wife
reads to Flapping Eagle from Virgil's diary of how Calf Island
was created and how Grimus plans to populate it with figures
from different dimensions. It serves as an acknowledgement of
the problems of cultural integration in society: 'Will there be a
problem in assimilating immigrants from these different planets
in the one society? Grimus is cheerfully optimistic. The differences

are too minute to matter, he says. I trust he is right' (*G*, 212).

Though peripheral in some ways to the admittedly obscure project of *Grimus*, the novel's treatment of women and of female sexuality is interesting in that its embrace of women's rights to social, political and sexual autonomy seems equally matched by a tendency to demonise female sexuality. If Rushdie's agenda for women is to depict their lives and loves without fear or favour, he seems curiously obliged always to demonstrate both rather than neither. In Liv Jones, we get the first of many 'ice-women' in his novels – someone who embodies a kind of crystalline perfection (in this case limited to Liv's beauty and sexual prowess) while at the same time maintaining the air of being unapproachable and unassailable. Both Farah Zoroaster in *Shame* and Allie Cone in *The Satanic Verses* have the epithet of ice-woman ascribed to them. With mysterious women such as Liv and Farah, this may simply be a way of depicting the distance they seem to desire between themselves and those, particularly the men, around them. But in a character as alive and 'explicable' as Allie Cone, it smacks of a perverse desire to establish the otherness of woman, particularly as a sexual being.

Similarly the use of the brothel as 'a place of refuge' (*G*, 133) in both *Grimus* and *The Satanic Verses* suggests the ambivalence if not outright confusion that Rushdie seems to feel when confronting overt manifestations of female sexuality. The 'tart with a heart' he so fondly depicts is as much a male construction as Islam's concepts of female purity and untouchability, so derided by him elsewhere. As with the image of the brothel, female sexuality contains both a promise and a threat. It is at once liberating as an expression of individual identity and oppressive in itself when it reminds man of his own weakness. In Flapping Eagle's journey through the Inner Dimension, the threat/promise dichotomy of female sexuality is embodied in Bird-Dog. Having been the woman who initiated him into the pleasures of sex, her body under Grimus's thrall becomes a labyrinthine tunnel, in a passage that displays the more disturbing traits in Rushdie's presentation of women:

The hole between her legs yawned: its hairs were like ropes. Ten yards away. She was a house, a cavern lying red and palpitating before him, the curtain of hair parting. He heard her booming voice. – Why resist, she was saying. Give up, little brother. Come in. Give up. Come in. (*G*, 71)

Later, when Flapping Eagle finally encounters Liv in her mountain retreat, she is shown to be dressed from head to toe in black, veiled, and with only slits for eye holes. As she sets about her sexual humiliation of the hero, she stands before him naked except for her veil. It is difficult not to associate her veil and robes with the *burqa* of Islam, protecting its women from the contaminating gaze of strangers – and her veiled nudity as a disturbing conflation of the sexually available and the sacrosanct.

The two women in the town of K who find their attention drawn to Flapping Eagle, Elfrida Gribb and Irina Cherkassova, in themselves represent this dichotomy: Irina, sexually rapacious and worldly; Elfrida, innocent and naive. It is arguable that Rushdie's treatment of women in later novels represents something more complex than a division between virgins and whores, but *Grimus* seems disturbingly simplistic in this respect. Much of the novel's sexual content is gratuitous, adding nothing to the storyline or the development of character (witness Virgil's oft-repeated, rather tedious breast fetish) while sexual degradation as a means of controlling women occurs too regularly for comfort. Whatever problems still adhere to Rushdie's treatment of women in his later novels, he is at least able to allegorise, politicise and humorise the sex according to demand. Here it is purely mechanised.

Rushdie's desire to draw on the genre of science fiction may account in part for some of the ingenuousness of the narrative, even perhaps for its presentation of women, sadly two-dimensional in much male science fiction. Rushdie says he turned to the genre because it was 'traditionally a good vehicle for the novel of ideas'.[19] But as Eric S. Rabkin points out, 'a good work of science fiction makes one and only one assumption about its narrative world that violates our knowledge about our own world and then extrapolates the whole narrative world from that difference.[20] This is clearly not the case with *Grimus*. Here, the reader is expected not only to suspend all normal narrative expectations and enter 'an other world', but also to be and remain as fully in tune with the real world, its literature, philosophies and religions as is intellectually possible. Rushdie is nothing if not a demanding read.

Rabkin posits the notion of a narrative continuum along which science fiction moves, embracing more and more elements of fantasy to take it away from the recognisable-but-not-quite-real situation of 'true' science fiction. Such 'technology' as appears in *Grimus*, most notably the powers of the Stone Rose, is clearly at the fantastic end of Rabkin's scale, while Rushdie's own working definition of science fiction as the novel of ideas would seem inadequate as a reason for employing the genre.

Elsewhere Rabkin speaks of the feelings of alienation and transformation that prompt much science fiction writing[21] and it is perhaps these moods that Rushdie is trying to recreate in *Grimus*. The alienation is not as yet politicised, the transformation is still more fantastic than social in nature. The desire to employ specific genres at this stage, however inappropriate they might ultimately prove, is perhaps a defence against the impending loss of narrative control that might come from the attempt to create the truly hybrid novel.

Grimus represents the beginning of a conception of literature as an orchestration of voices – one in which the art of the oriental storyteller is blended with a diversity of literary techniques to form something entirely individual. The 'bagginess' of *Grimus*'s narrative is of a different nature to that of, say, *Midnight's Children*. One can accept Elfrida Gribb's views on narrative without feeling that Rushdie successfully implemented them in the novel: 'I do not care for stories that are so, so tight. Stories should be like life, slightly frayed at the edges, full of loose ends and lives juxtaposed by accident rather than some grand design.' (*G*, 141)

Grimus is clearly a product of a period when Rushdie had not yet achieved the synthesis of diverse cultural strands and narrative forms. He rightly attributes the text's failure to this lack of a defined voice at its heart, or even, to borrow from Sufism, a unified voice which expresses its own diversity : 'I feel very distant from [*Grimus*], mainly because I don't like the language it is written in. It's a question of hearing your own voice, and I don't hear it because I hadn't found it then.'[22]

Midnight's Children

RUSHDIE regarded *Grimus* as an attempt at amalgamating both the eastern and the western influences on his writing: '[I] wanted to find a way of taking themes out of Oriental thought and expressing them in a western novel.'[1] It is noticeable that at this stage of his development Rushdie conceives of his 'project' as the injection of 'eastern content' into an unchanged 'western form' (the novel). The reason for *Grimus*'s failure is that this graft does not take. Rushdie's later work demonstrates a growing awareness that the introduction of new content must be accompanied by a change in form. Indeed, Saleem Sinai declares in *Midnight's Children* that 'There is no escape from form.' (*MC*, 226) In order to admit eastern themes, the western novel form must mutate and develop to become something else entirely; the hybrid post-colonial text. This chapter will focus on the ways in which *Midnight's Children*, published some six years after *Grimus*, achieves a successful fusion of east and west in terms of both form *and* content.

During a lecture in Denmark in 1983, Rushdie reflected on the power of Indian oral storytellers to draw huge crowds and hold the undivided attention of their largely illiterate audiences.[2] He indicated his desire to capture some of the feel of such an oral performance within the textual confines of *Midnight's Children*. This represented a significant acknowledgement of the influence of eastern exponents and intertexts on his particular brand of narrative. Up to this point, the names most often on Rushdie's lips in the roles of acknowledged influences on his work stretch no further east in origin than Russia: Rabelais, Joyce, Dickens, Gogol, Boccaccio, Kafka.[3]

However, it is necessary to ask whether Rushdie's claim of a relationship between his writing and oral narrative is anything more than a desire to forge a link with his cultural heritage? The question of how deeply a text can be said to be imbued with a sense of orality is hard to assess. One can find written expressions or versions of the oral, as is the case with *The Thousand and One Nights*, but the notion of reproducing oral narratives through writing becomes, on one level, a contradiction in terms.

Perhaps a more productive way of posing the question would be to ask – does an understanding of the techniques of an oral storyteller contribute to our understanding of the form of *Midnight's Children*? Using Walter J. Ong's study of the relation between oral and print cultures, *Orality and Literacy*,[4] it is possible to trace some suggestive correspondences. For example, Ong explains how oral narratives such as the Ancient Greek form of epic, the products of a primary oral culture, never proceeded to develop linear plots, and that Horace's injunction to begin *in medias res* (literally 'in the middle of things') had more to do with necessity than a deliberate diversification from an established norm.

Rushdie's hero, Saleem Sinai, draws our attention to sequentiality in the narrative of *Midnight's Children*, when he reaches the 'story's half-way point, one that reeks of beginnings and ends, when you could say it should be more concerned with middles'. (*MC*, 223) A chronological approach to such complex narratives as the epic poems would lead to too many errors and omissions. Ong's assessment of the skill of the epic poet lends some weight to Rushdie's claim of affinities between *Midnight's Children* and earlier oral narrative structures. According to Ong, the good epic poet displays the:

> tacit acceptance of the fact that episodic structure was the only way and the totally natural way of imagining and handling lengthy narrative, and, second, possession of supreme skill in managing flashbacks and other episodic techniques.[5]

Midnight's Children draws on the models of the seemingly endless and digressive Indian epics the *Mahabharata* and

Ramayana, those 'interminable tales' already referred to by Raja Rao in the introduction to this study. With its thirty chapters or 'jars' of pickled personal and national history, its meandering digressions and metronomic swings through time and space, *Midnight's Children* illustrates a link between Rushdie's chosen style of communication in the text and the forms of oral narrative that he seeks to reproduce.

Those same forms also provide Saleem Sinai with a way of organising his own complex autobiography. He is literally 'handcuffed to history' (*MC,* 9) – the circumstances of his own birth making him analogous to the newly emergent independent nation of India. His narrative is therefore simultaneously the story of his own life and a mirror of the life of India itself. Saleem significantly eschews a purely linear, chronological mode of narration in favour of one which veers between past, present and future, presaging not only the arrival of events and characters which will later be revealed, but also his own annihilation.

Like Laurence Sterne's *Tristram Shandy,* an influence acknowledged by Rushdie,[6] Saleem relates a substantial part of his personal and family history before he finally gets round to describing his own birth. He leads us backwards and forwards in time between his present standpoint of 1978, back to the events of his father Aadam's childhood, down through the intervening years to the simultaneous birth of himself and of free India. The model for this pendulum movement in the narrative is what Saleem calls 'the metronome music of Mountbatten's countdown calendar' to independence (*MC,* 106). The metronomic beat of the tick-tock of Saleem's time-scale not only leads the narrative to midnight on August 14–15 1947, but also provides the model for its movement from the outset. Just as a metronome or pendulum picks up the speed and regularity of its beat from the initially wider swing which provides it with its momentum, so the narrative intermittently takes a swing further back into family and national history before resuming its steady tick-tock drift between two historical points.

The complexity of oral narrative, with its swoops, spirals, digression and reiteration, can therefore be seen as the perfect

correlative of Rushdie's technique in *Midnight's Children*. Both
the novel and its Indian oral models set out to give the impression of random construction, but it is a pretence belied by the
eventual pattern of these narratives. Though ultimately exer-
cising supreme control over the different directions in which the
narrative is pulled, Saleem is in constant fear that his story will,
like his own cracking body, disintegrate into tiny, unreconstruc-
table pieces. He is obliged by the internal compulsion of his own
story to reach a certain point in history and the narrative, while
his omniscience allows him to meddle with and distort both.
Such internal compulsion is provided in one way by the physical
movement of people and events in the text as they edge nearer to
a central position in the storyteller's consciousness: 'Tai is getting
nearer. He who revealed the power of the nose, and who is now
bringing my grandfather the message which will catapult him
into his future, is stroking his shikara through the early morning
lake…' (*MC*, 14).

Time also exerts its authority over Saleem both within and
outside his narrative. Just as the seconds tick down to midnight
for India, so Saleem, pursued and compelled by the demands of
his critic-within-the-text Padma and the cracks that threaten his
disintegration, is forced like Scheherazade to preserve his very
existence through the continuation of his narrative (*MC*, 9 and
24). Nancy E. Batty provides an illuminating discussion of the art
of suspense as practised in *Midnight's Children*, and Rushdie's
deliberate invocation of Scheherazade's plight at the hands of
King Shahryar in *The Thousand and One Nights*, whom she
must keep continuously entertained by her stories if she is to
save her own life.[7]

Just as Rushdie proclaimed the value and appeal of storytelling for Indian audiences, so the figures of illiterate producers
and consumers of stories are introduced into the body of *Midnight's Children* in the forms of Tai and Padma. Tai the boatman
is also a storyteller, spinner of yarns and inhabiter of fantasies,
who mirrors in his own 'technique' the formal construction of
Saleem's narrative and the novel as a whole with his 'magical
talk, words pouring from him like fools' money… soaring up to

the most remote Himalayas of the past, then swooping shrewdly on some present detail… to vivisect its meaning like a mouse' (*MC*, 15).

While Tai is able to spellbind the young Aadam Aziz with his tales, Padma is a vital spur and judge of Saleem's autobiography; his 'necessary ear' (*MC*, 149). Her temporary departure from Saleem's house threatens to give his story the one thing she felt it lacked and which he had strongly resisted. Her absence presents him with the prospect of a narrative strait-jacket; a descent into 'the narrow one-dimensionality of a straight line' (*MC*, 150) rather than the continuous ebb and flow between past and present, 'pulling away' from events 'in a long rising spiral' (*MC*, 103).

In many ways, Padma's role in *Midnight's Children* is representative of the separate technical and even cultural demands that writing the novel made on Rushdie. On the one hand, she can be seen as the exemplification of Roland Barthes's arguments on the role of the reader subsequent to the 'death' of the author – 'that someone who holds together in a single field all the traces by which the written text is constituted'[8] apparently affirming the text's status as postmodern production. On the other, she provides a link back to the culture which Rushdie insists informs his work most strongly. Padma, taken on these terms, becomes a vocal and individualised member of the multitude which sits at the feet of the storyteller, hanging on his every word.

Nancy E. Batty argues that 'Padma's role as Saleem's "necessary ear" should not obscure her status as co-creator of his narrative.'[9] Batty sees the relating of Saleem's tale to Padma as a form of seduction where consummation is deferred for as long as possible. 'Saleem tailors his narrative for Padma: like a lover engaged in making a sexual conquest, Saleem adjusts his strategies of seduction according to the response which those strategies elicit.'[10]

A further consideration which links both the issues of orality and Padma's role in the text relates to the extent to which the individual listening to the discourse of a storyteller coincides with the position occupied by the reader of a text. Walter Ong argues that there is a crucial difference between the position of 'listener' and that of 'reader' observing:

> Spoken utterance is addressed by a real, living person or… persons, at a specific time in a real setting… Yet words are alone in a text. More-over, … in 'writing' something, the one producing the written utterance is also alone.[11]

Establishing Rushdie's conception of the reader within and outside his texts requires one to piece together often conflicting opinions. Writing just after the publication and success of *Midnight's Children*, Rushdie declared that he had never had a particular reader in mind, and had merely hoped that the finished product would be of interest to others (*IH*, 19). Eight years later, at the height of the furore over *The Satanic Verses*, the reader of a Rushdie text is characterised as being drawn into a symbiotic relationship with the writer, where the reader is involved in the text and colludes in the very act of creativity (*IH*, 426). It is a complex and dramatic view of the act of creation-through-interpretation performed by the reader of a text. The creation of this 'unique' work is, of course, problematised by the fact that reader and writer can come to widely differing conclusions about what the text actually says.

Questioned specifically on the reader/writer relation the following year, Rushdie is again explicit about the writer's solitude as characterised by Ong, indicating that in the act of writing he has no sense of an audience and is only conscious of his own solitude.[12] He goes on to say that an awareness of possible readers and their responses can arise subsequent to the act of creation. The reader in such a context becomes a moveable feast, occupying a shifting position both in relation to the text itself and as he or she is envisaged by the writer. These are important considerations when assessing who exactly Rushdie is writing 'for'.

Padma's role within the text is clearly a symbolic one. She becomes critical of the processes of construction and reconstitution of personal and national history in which the text is engaged. She is not merely a symbol of the Indian storyteller's audience – its captivity or credulity crystallised into a single identity – but a symbol also of a wider critical position in relation to the narrative mode itself. As with Rushdie's treatment of factual error in the relating of historical incident, which will be discussed later, Padma serves to embody a critical scepticism about the narrative and to suggest a relationship of contestation between the text's form and content. As Keith Wilson puts it in his essay '*Midnight's Children* and Reader Responsibility': 'out of the distance between his readers and Padma, Rushdie makes the "meaning" that Saleem can only, frenetically, hope to find'.[13] It is through Padma's eyes that we are made aware of our own difficulties in dealing with the demands of the text.

One of the formal strengths of *Midnight's Children* is the way in which through its disrupted narrative, Rushdie makes the reader acutely aware of the important part played by his or her own memory in 'reconstructing' the text as meaningful narrative. Memory as the key to constructing narrative is fragile, and unwilling to obey external demands made upon it. In his essay '"Errata" or Unreliable Narration in *Midnight's Children*', Rushdie recalls his own surprise that he had not in fact been in India during one of her border wars, despite his memory of events convincing him that this was the case (*IH*, 24). The same is true of Saleem's recollection of India's 1957 elections, placing them after his tenth birthday rather than before. The demands Saleem makes on his memory are enormous – the process of remembering must be made to speed up, so as not to be overtaken by his own physical disintegration. This forefronting of memory dictates the form of the narrative. Rushdie's essay on the errata in the text can be read differently in the light of this – less as a description of a postmodern artist's exploration of unreliable narration than an illustration of the 'erratic' processes by which the migrant's sense of history reconstitutes itself *through* memory.

Indeed, one of the chief achievements of *Midnight's Children* is the way in which it serves as a testament to the importance of memory in the recreation of history and the constitution of the individual's identity. As Saleem puts it, 'morality, judgment, character... it all starts with memory' (*MC*, 381). It is Parvati's memory of Saleem which gives him back his name, and the memory of his former life symbolised by the spittoon that keeps him in touch with that newly rediscovered identity. Rushdie describes a similar process where he himself experienced a restoration of the past to him through memory. The sight of an old black and white photograph of his childhood home in Bombay created in him the desire to re-imagine that past and restore it to himself (*IH*, 10).

Rushdie admits that the act of reclaiming the past is subject to the vagaries of the memory on which its reconstruction relies. His essay on unreliable narration in *Midnight's Children* is a study of the tricks which memory plays on the writer attempting to recall the past, and also of the tricks the writer can play on the reader in the name of unreliability (*IH*, 22–5). By confusing us as to why certain incorrect details have been included in the narrative – through genuine authorial error, through the desire to indicate the subjective nature of Saleem's recollections, or to allow information to fall somewhere between the two – Rushdie is able to forefront memory itself as an integral feature of his depiction of India, and to make the subject of the novel 'the way in which we remake the past to suit our present purposes, using memory as our tool' (*IH*, 24).

The 'intentional' error arising from the date of Gandhi's assassination in the text is a case in point. Rushdie, through Saleem, seems to be toying with the idea of how much control one can exert over even misleading chronology and how much this ultimately matters. In terms of history as it affects the individual, it does not matter *when* Gandhi was assassinated, only that he *was*, and how this impinged on the individual and collective consciousnesses of Indian citizens. Saleem's statement that Gandhi will continue to die at the wrong time in 'his' India (*MC*, 166) draws attention to the passage of time in which the reader reads the text and not the more abstract, because distanced, concept of historical chronology. On rereading the novel, Gandhi will always die at the wrong time and the error will always be pointed out after the fact. The answer to the question posed to the reader by Saleem, 'Does one error invalidate the

entire fabric?' (*MC*, 166) has to be 'no' when considered from
this angle.

Rushdie's project as stated in his essay 'Imaginary Homelands' was to depict post-independence India in such a way that it
displayed human history *as it appears to the individual*, with all
the confusion that that implies. Indeed, within the novel, Saleem
explains the different relations of the individual to history with
all the pompous pontification of Polonius addressing Hamlet on
styles of acting; the 'passive-metaphorical', 'passive-literal',
'active-metaphorical' and so on (*MC*, 238). Saleem's 'literal'
interventions in history are moments such as that when he rides
into the language marchers on his bicycle and literally collides
with history and alters the course of events.

How the western reader sees his/her position in this scenario is
debatable. Rushdie speaks with evident amusement of the Indian
readers who rebuked him with the novel's 'errors' in Hindu
mythology and bus-timetabling and says we should entertain 'a
healthy distrust' (*IH*, 25) of Saleem's narrative. But it may be
that Rushdie's obvious erudition creates a textual double-bind
here which also returns us to the question of an implied audience. Would the 'average' western reader of a Rushdie novel
know that Ganesh acted as amanuensis to Vyasa in the creation
of the *Mahabharata* and not to Valmiki in that of the
Ramayana? Timothy Brennan, for example, falls over himself to
suggest that this is a 'variation of the myth' of Ganesh's involvement, apparently failing completely to pick up on Rushdie's 'in-
joke'.[14] Or maybe this is in itself proof of Rushdie's arguments
that individual recollections and assessments of history or reality
as a whole are ultimately self-validating. Individual versions of
reality provide a version of 'truth' for the individual.

The art of memory is itself constructed around the objects
and artefacts which come to represent its fabric in the narrative.
This is closely bound up with Rushdie's adoption of leitmotifs in
the text – a 'non-rational network of connections'[15] which carries
with it a cumulative rather than symbolic weight. The silver spittoon is one of the chief of these, helping to crystallise Saleem's
sense of his personal history, as previously stated. Like the

formulaic and repeated phrases of ancient epic poetry which help
the poet to locate his position in the recounting of the narrative,
the spittoons, washing chests, globes and perforated sheets of
Saleem's past, map out his memory of growing up alongside the
new India. The letter from Nehru celebrating the illustrious
moment of his birth and the photograph of himself as a baby
from the *Times of India* are preserved for posterity inside
Saleem's old tin globe and buried in the garden of Buckingham
Villa before the family's final departure for Pakistan. This episode is mirrored in an account in Ved Mehta's book *A Family
Affair* of the discovery of Mrs Gandhi's own desire that posterity
should remember her:

> In the first summer of Janata rule, politicians, and officials
> were gossiping and tittering about a ten-thousand-word
> document that had been encased in steel and buried forty
> feet underground at the Red Fort... The document was a
> time capsule that had been prepared by Mrs Gandhi's gov-
> ernment at a cost of thirty thousand rupees... and it con-
> tained an account of Indian history from Independence...
> through August 15, 1972.[16]

It is one of the occasions where Saleem's remembered history intersects with that of the 'official' textbook versions. The
flying spittoon which brains Saleem at the end of Book Two and
'liberates' him from his past by inducing a state of amnesia, occasions a loss which is more than a loss of memory. For Saleem to
lose his memory is to lose his identity; his link with the past
which places him in the social and historical context that outlines
his individuality. Memory is the chain which connects the post-
colonial subject to his or her disrupted history.

The text also makes use of other individual recollections of
history. References in the text which might otherwise slip past
unnoted as mere embellishments of Saleem's narrative are in fact
instances of just such a borrowing. References to 'Mountbatten's
countdown calendar' (*MC*, 106) mentioned earlier, and his wife's
secret consumption of chicken breasts in a locked lavatory (*MC*,
65) demonstrate how the reality of history-in-the-making bears
its own resemblances to the absurdities and incongruities of the

fictionalised process. Larry Collins and Dominique Lapierre in *Freedom At Midnight* give accounts of the actual events that gave rise to these two images. Edwina Mountbatten, on arriving at Viceroy's House and asking for food for her dogs, was amazed when roasted chicken breasts were brought for them. Apalled at this decadence, she took the chicken herself, and ate it, locked in her bathroom.[17] Her husband's desire for efficiency in the hasty arrangements for Independence led him to construct:

> a rip-off day to day calendar which he ordered displayed in offices everywhere in Delhi. Like a countdown to an explosion, a large red square in the middle of each page of the calendar registered the number of days left to 15 August.[18]

But if Saleem is as handcuffed to history as he claims, then memory and its artefacts are as important to the nation's sense of itself as they are to the individual. In his essay 'In God We Trust', Rushdie praises Benedict Anderson's study *Imagined Communities: Reflections on the Origins and Spread of Nationalism*[19] for supporting the view (inherent in Saleem's narrative) that 'the idea of sequence, of narrative, of society as a story, is essential to the creation of nations' (*IH*, 382). Saleem reinforces the idea of the imagined community when he speaks of India as a country dreamed into existence by 'a phenomenal act of collective will' (*MC*, 112). If the nation itself is an imagined construct, then nationalism and a sense of national identity seem also to be products of individual and collective will.

Saleem's embrace of Pakistani citizenship at the beginning of Book Three is seen as an act of submission. Nationalism in this instance becomes an embrace of non-identity. Saleem's lack of consciousness as he becomes a tracker dog for the Pakistani military leads to a split in him which mirrors Pakistan's own split as it divides to form Bangladesh. This can be seen as an important stage in the development of the argument of *The Satanic Verses*, that a lack of consciousness of, or belief in, one's identity can be a specific by-product of colonialism. In contrast, Saleem sees the Brass Monkey's newly constructed stage personality of Jamila

Singer as a by-product of emergent Pakistani nationalism. Her patriotism in the land of the pure is counterpoised by Saleem's ability to sniff out the seedier side of life, away from the virtues of nationalistic fervour. Aadam Aziz and Saleem both suffer from the gaps in their identities left by the god-shaped hole, while the national identity of Pakistan uses religion as the 'glue' to hold itself together (*MC*, 351).

As for the political make-up of the nation, there is a tension in *Midnight's Children* between the desire to explore heroism and individuality on the one hand and the attraction of the collectivist politics of such figures as Mian Abdullah and Picture Singh on the other. The novel illustrates the complexity of Rushdie's position – he achieves the individualisation of Saleem's identity *through* his very relation to the social units of family and community. Saleem is as handcuffed to society as he is to history. *Midnight's Children* differs from *Grimus* and prefigures *Shame* in its level of engagement with the realities of political life and in particular the abuses attendant on the assumption of dictatorial power. Rushdie's depiction of Indira Gandhi as 'the Black Widow' locates her simultaneously as historical reality and monstrous fantasy.

As with the later 'veiled' figures of Bhutto and Zia of Pakistan in *Shame*, the representation of Indira Gandhi seems subject to the liberal Manichaeism at the heart of his political pronouncements. Perhaps exhibiting a debt to popular culture once again, Rushdie likes his villains to be recognisably and unequivocally villainous – set out in black and white terms (or in Indira's case 'No colours except green and black' (*MC*, 207)) in defiance of their actual complexity. Without doubting the sincerity of Rushdie's views on the abuses of the Emergency period, it is depressing, for instance, that Indira's villainy is represented in such relentlessly misogynistic terms. It is interesting, as Katherine Frank points out in her article 'Mr Rushdie and Mrs Gandhi'[20] that Indira Gandhi's libel suit against Rushdie and the first edition of *Midnight's Children* centred on the suggestion that she had hastened her husband Feroze's early death from a heart attack. She won the case and the offending comments were removed from subsequent editions. Rushdie may congratulate himself that she did not take him to court to contest her sanctioning of Emergency horrors, but it is also important to recognise the age-old misogynist mythology that condemns the Hindu widow as bad luck and a social non-person, traditionally condemned to a life of isolation if not coerced into being burned alive on her husband's funeral pyre. Why situate Saleem's torture in the widow's hostel in Benares except to play into the hands of this myth?

An issue related to the representation of 'real' historical figures in Rushdie's writing, and which will be returned to in the discussion of *Shame*, is the relationship and possible conflict between realism and fantasy not only as modes of representation but as categories of 'reality' in themselves. The question of perspective is always at the centre of Rushdie's debates on the literary and non-literary constructions of reality. Partly it is a play on the Hindu concept of *maya* – the illusory quality of what we perceive to be reality or the world – and partly a slight parody of the adoption of this concept by British writers in their representations of India. Much of the action of Paul Scott's *Raj Quartet*, which so irritated Rushdie in his essay 'Outside the Whale', takes place in the 'imagined' India of the aptly named Mayapore, while Rushdie mocks Forster's India by offering us his own 'Dr Aziz' in the form of Saleem's grandfather, Aadam. Indeed, Rushdie saw writing *Midnight's Children* as a way of breaking away from Western depictions of India.[21]

Rushdie's use of the cinema screen in *Midnight's Children* as a metaphor for the illusion/reality split can be seen on one level as a debunking of the quasi-mystical language sometimes adopted by such writers as Forster and Scott to convey that aspect of Indian 'reality' which they cannot comprehend or assimilate into their existing view of the world. To question the nature of perception through the brash artificiality of the Bombay talkies is to introduce a new dimension into the discussion, perhaps specifically chosen to jar with the abstraction of the Marabar caves in *A Passage to India* or the romanticised attitudes of many of Scott's characters.

Ashis Nandy writes in his essay 'Satyajit Ray's Secret Guide' that

> Only a handful of writers has matched the insight with
> which Rushdie speaks in *Midnight's Children* of elements
> of the new popular culture in urban India such as Bombay
> films and professional wrestling bouts entering the inter-
> stices of the middle-class worldview.[22]

Saleem states that 'nobody from Bombay should be without a
basic film vocabulary' (*MC*, 33) and his own familiarity with the
conventions of Bollywood gained as a member of the Metro Cub
Club is put to use not only in constructing his narrative but also
in colouring and interpreting that action for us. Thus he uses
close-ups or long-shots to situate the reader in relation to the
action, while he spies on Nadir Khan and Amina acting out their
illicit liaison like censored screen lovers (*MC*, 217). The lines that
separate the filmic from the real begin to blur.

The 'real' and the fantastic are similarly overlaid in the text
by its relation of characters to mythical archetypes within the
Hindu pantheon. Both Saleem and in turn his 'son' Aadam are
associated with the elephant-headed god Ganesh, son of Shiva
and Parvati in Hindu mythology. The textual Shiva is Saleem's
alter ego but is also representative of the Hindu god of destruction who needs his female counterpart Parvati in order to create.
Saleem, like Rushdie, is a Muslim, but both are 'well up in Hindu
stories' (*MC*, 149).

If, by virtue of these mythic and filmic elements, reality
itself becomes questionable in the text, then realism as a mode of
representation of reality becomes equally open to examination.
Different narrative techniques are effectively debated in the text
of *Midnight's Children*. Saleem's film-making uncle Hanif
discovers a passion for realistic screenplays to set against the
mythical, fantastic preoccupations of the Bombay film industry.
These debates ultimately lead into the argument around which
literary form is best suited to the depiction of a new democracy
emerging from beneath the yoke of colonialism.

Midnight's Children shows that subversions of realism can
be used as much for the purposes of oppression as liberation.
Saleem's arch rival Shiva adopts the 'technique' of inverting the
emotional responses that would normally attach to certain

situations. Murders are thus described casually, while a good hand of cards is cause for poetic licence. He is engaged in creating alternative realities of a sort, in that his distance from the object or situation viewed colours his perception of it. The problem is that his own psychosis means he is unable to distinguish between events and get close enough to perceive the realities of the murder.

The metaphorical nature of language, and the question of how far language can be a bar to communication, are both explored in *Midnight's Children*. Rushdie enjoys playing with the literal and metaphorical meanings of different phrases – Ahmed Sinai's 'frozen assets'; the failing business venture symbolised by his icy testicles, and the declining standard of Amina Brand towels which force his wife literally to air her dirty laundry in private (*MC*, 157). In one instance, the shift from the literal to the metaphoric is plotted for us by Saleem. Facing financial ruin following the collapse of his land reclamation programme, Ahmed Sinai is further tormented by plans to alter the system of texation, complaining that the government is going to the bathroom all over the people. 'He stomped off', declares Saleem, 'leaving me with a clear understanding of what people meant when they said the country was going to pot' (*MC*, 201). It serves as a possible explanation of one of English's many cryptic phrases while at the same time redefining it – an example of the Indianisation or Rushdification of English.

Language is also shown to be a site of conflict in the novel in the form of language riots between Marathi and Gujerati speakers. Importantly, Saleem chooses to communicate with the other children of midnight in a way which reaches beyond this site of conflict – inhabiting their consciousnesses directly. But like the Indian storyteller, Saleem is not merely a 'transmitter' but a creative artist who imposes his personality on the form of communication, which eventually comes to reflect rather than negate the author/creator's centrality.

The discussion of invisibility within the text can also be seen as crucial to the question of the post-colonial writer's relationship to the society s/he observes. Invisibility can be a political necessity. The poet Nadir Khan fears for his life following the murder of Mian Abdullah, seeking refuge in the cellar of Aadam Aziz's house. Invisibility is also the refuge of the voyeur as well as the political exile. Saleem as post-colonial artist becomes the spectator on the periphery of society, able to view the actions of others, in his washing chest or concealed in the clocktower, because he is literally or socially invisible. This tension between observation and voyeurism becomes even more explicit in *Shame*, but in *Midnight's Children* invisibility does at least allow Saleem to reflect on the nature of his narrative. When he hides from Nadir Khan and Amina, he knows that he is the 'director' controlling our view of the 'actors'. As with the rest of the narrative, we are left to contemplate the carefully staged construction of Saleem's account of history. The text demonstrates that control is not an illusion but is vitally important for maintaining an authorial or creative identity.

Parvati's role in securing Saleem's safe return to India from Bangladesh in Book Three links the question of invisibility in the novel with the idea of woman as refuge which is a recurring feature of Rushdie's texts. Parvati's wicker basket enables her to make men disappear until she wills them to return. It is yet another 'basket of invisibility' (*MC*, 385) for Saleem, but one where, far from being empowered, he is instead preserved in a curious state of limbo. The situation differs from his concealment in the washing chest in that it is controlled by a woman. Like the brothels in *Grimus* and *The Satanic Verses*, women and female sexuality are both the refuge and the abyss, and Saleem fears that Parvati's basket will send him into oblivion. Paradoxically, however, Parvati is also the agent for restoring Saleem's identity to him. By recognising him, she effectively gives him back the name he has forgotten.

Names are again crucial in *Midnight's Children* and Parvati shares with other characters in the text and with Flapping Eagle in *Grimus* the fact of a voluntary change of identity through the assumption of a new name. Parvati becomes Laylah, Mumtaz becomes Amina and Nadir Khan becomes Qasim the Red. This insistence on the pliable and reconstructable nature of identity has particular significance within the context of post-colonial literature. Just as some artists and intellectuals share the writer Nayantara Sahgal's resistance to the idea that colonisation represents the most important determinant of personal and national identity,[23] so the depiction of figures who reinvent themselves can serve as a positive refutation that the past is the place where character and fate are decided. 'Our names contain our fates' Saleem tells us (*MC*, 304), but a change of name, the assertion of identity as fluid, means that the individual's fate need not be once and forever determined.

Saleem's own name is itself an index of so many of Rushdie's preoccupations, mirroring as it does that of Ibn Sina, 'master magician, Sufi adept' (*MC*, 304). Here in *Midnight's Children*, the identity of the post-colonial subject is inseparably linked to that of the nation itself while in his next work, *Shame*, the nation takes precedence over the centrality of any one individual. The formation of positively fluid and hybrid identities will continue to be of paramount importance in all Rushdie's subsequent fiction, perhaps nowhere more so than in *The Satanic Verses*. In terms of his own life, Rushdie can be seen to be following a clear if not entirely consciously envisaged journey through elements of his own multifaceted identity with the chronology of his novels – from east to west, from Bombay to Ellowen Deeowen. *Midnight's Children* returned his Indian past to him while *Shame* leads on to the Rushdie family's own destination, Pakistan.

At the start of this chapter it was argued that *Midnight's Children* represented an important moment in Rushdie's development. His western audience had been startled by this display of literary fireworks and had made the assumption that such a talent must be 'coming from' two places at once – providing them with a taste of the orient in a western form.[24] It is noticeable that following the publication of *Midnight's Children* Rushdie's awareness of his relation to earlier Indian writing in English, shifts towards one of greater acceptance.

Part of the difficulty Rushdie seems to have experienced in locating his writing may stem from the tension between embracing or refuting the notion of an Indian 'tradition' in writing. In his essay '"Commonwealth Literature" Does Not Exist', Rushdie asks

how critics can speak of an Indian tradition when Indianness itself defies categorisation by virtue of its heterogeneity and
diversity. But in the same year he is telling the audience at his
Danish lecture that he wishes to speak about 'the sense in which
[*Midnight's Children*] derives out of an Indian tradition'.[25] He
clearly argues for the existence and continuance of a distinct oral
tradition in Indian culture, exemplified in this instance by the
crowd-pulling storyteller of Baroda to whom he refers.

One criticism which can be levelled at *Midnight's Children*,
regarded by so many as Rushdie's finest work, is a lack of sub-
tlety in some of its features. Wary on the one hand of falling prey
to the 'Indian disease'; the 'urge to encapsulate the whole of
reality' (*MC*, 75), Saleem, and beyond him Rushdie, nevertheless attempts it. It is as if the novels that follow *Midnight's
Children* have slowed the hectic pace of ideas, curbed the somewhat contradictory impulses of his writing (what claim can a
'dead' author make for the necessity and excellence of post-
colonial writing?), and led to the production of texts which
ultimately *say* more, with greater coherence. Like the magicians
of Picture Singh's ghetto, Rushdie in *Midnight's Children* asks
us to admire the display of literary fireworks, conjuring tricks
and fantastic items pulled from the artist's hat. But a narrowing
of the focus, an antidote to the Indian disease, produces a more
powerful, because more condensed, effect.

There is a suggestion in *Midnight's Children* itself of
Rushdie's awareness of this fact. Saleem's plea to the children of
midnight is to establish an identity particular to themselves and
their condition which is not conceived in purely negative, reac-
tive terms: an identity that falls between the unproductive
dualisms inherent in social divisions. Such an argument for a
middle path when applied to the text itself demonstrates an
awareness on Rushdie's part, however vague at this stage, that
the fully hybridised text can and must fall between the extremes
of postmodern plurality on the one hand and the desire to root
narrative within national specifics on the other.

Shame

As the previous chapter indicated, form asserts itself as a crucial consideration in any assessment of *Midnight's Children*. By comparison, *Shame* is a model of closed construction, very different from both the digressive 'baggy monster' which preceded it and from *The Satanic Verses* that was yet to come. *Shame* is aware of its narrative trajectory from the outset. Peter Brigg, in his study of the text, speaks of 'the presence of destiny which sees all of the elements of the plot dovetail into a coherent pattern'.[1] From the umbilical cord wrapped around the neck of Raza Hyder's dead child (*S*, 82), to the noose around the neck of Hyder's deposed rival (*S*, 238), the cyclical pattern of the imagery is clear and unwavering.

As with Rushdie's other fictional enterprises, it is a case of content dictating form. The nature of his arguments demands representation and explication through forms which display a corresponding tone, whether of chaos, confusion, fantasy or moral and political didacticism. Rushdie desires to tell a cautionary tale about the Pakistani élite in *Shame* – a tale that demonstrates the numerous ills bred by oppression and in which violence and corruption gain their just rewards – and it is this internal compulsion that contributes to the impression of the text as closed, bearing a predetermined argument.

The blend of fairy-tale and hard-hitting social realism which characterises both *Midnight's Children* and *The Satanic Verses* is handled less deftly in *Shame*. It neither creates the psychological 'reality' of *The Satanic Verses* nor does it have the characteristic exuberance of *Midnight's Children*. It is by attention to the structural differences between *Shame* and Rushdie's other novels, and the structural 'options' that the text rehearses, that one can judge the problems that still adhere to what, on the surface, is a more clearly envisaged and executed literary enterprise than its predecessor.

'When a tyrant falls, the world's shadows lighten, and only hypocrites grieve... ' wrote Rushdie at the news of General Zia Ul-Haq's death in a plane crash in 1988 (*IH*, 53). Rushdie's attitude to the styles of government of Zia and his predecessor Zulfikar Ali Bhutto is as evident in the construction of *Shame* as in his non-fictional outpourings in the name of democracy and free speech. At the centre of his allegory of Pakistani society move the figures of Bhutto and Zia, only thinly disguised by the veil thrown across them. So thin is this disguise that Rushdie has always attempted to deny that Arjumand 'Virgin Ironpants' Harappa, daughter of his Bhutto figure, Iskander Harappa, is modelled on Bhutto's daughter Benazir – a political animal in her own right and chief bearer of the sacred flame of her executed father's memory.[2] In *The Jaguar Smile*, Rushdie writes that 'Benazir Bhutto... referred to her dead father in every public speech. (She called him *Shaheed sahib*, Mr Martyr.)'.[3]

Aside from the thorny question of intentionality raised by Rushdie's disclaimer is the confusion apparent in his own pronouncements on the text concerning its form and structure. In one interview he calls *Shame* a 'realistic' novel,[4] in another it is 'not entirely a *roman-à-clef*'.[5] Similarly the setting for the novel is both 'slightly fantasized',[6] while 'behind the fantasized or mythologized country in the book there is a real country'.[7] It is this fact of parallel 'realities' in the text – the fictional nation and its dictatorial oligarchy overlaying but never obscuring their 'factual' counterparts – and the arguments that are generated by the fictional realities, that dictate its structure. The imperatives behind and within its conception (for instance, Rushdie's own statement that 'the book is set in Pakistan and it deals, centrally, with the way in which the sexual repressions of that country are connected to the political repressions'[8]) contribute to what is, after *Midnight's Children*, an increased feeling of predetermination in the text.

The shift in perspective from the panoramic sweep of *Midnight's Children* to the channelled focus of *Shame*'s gaze is reflected in the reader's relationship to the text's central figure. Where Saleem Sinai called upon us to see him as occupying a central position in the history of post-independence India – if not, in some instances, as the very motor of its progress – the narrator of *Shame* asks us to view Omar Khayyam Shakil, the text's putative hero, as 'a creature of the edge: a peripheral man' (*S*, 24). Omar's name is intended to recall that of the Persian poet, Umar Khayyam[9] known in the West for his *Rubaiyyat* or quatrains translated by Edward Fitzgerald in the nineteenth century. As Brennan points out, Umar Khayyam is significant not just because he was himself reputedly a man of science, as is Omar, but because doubts also exist as to his authorship of all the quatrains, making Umar a figure peripheral in one sense to his own fame. Other literary artefacts discovered by Omar in his grandfather's library reinforce Rushdie's central image of the 'artist' dissociated from his work – Burton's translation of the *Alf Laylah wa laylah* (*The Thousand and One Nights*) and the poems of Ibn Battuta, a wandering figure whose work may again be unreliable in its authorship.[10]

Here in *Shame* the notions of heroism and individuality explored in *Midnight's Children* are examined in relation to a man of dubious personal and moral integrity. Indeed the very shift of focus away from and then back to Omar demonstrates his peripheral position in the text itself. Born in his grandfather's death-bed to an apparent triumvirate of mothers, Omar is assailed from the outset by contradictions and inversions; birth and death, the real and the fantastic. The 'world turned upside-down' (*S*, 21) which he appears to inhabit threatens to plunge him into a void, a nightmarish existence where such a birth and such a childhood presage annihilation of identity.

In an attempt to lift the threat of this disintegration, Omar assumes an illusory or dream persona, one which the narrative voice refuses to pin down as either good or evil; either 'caped crusader or cloaked blood-sucker.' (*S*, 22) Once again, as in *Midnight's Children* and his lecture 'Is Nothing Sacred?', Rushdie plays with the idea of the secret identity behind which both writers and ordinary mortals hide, reinforcing the sense of their exceptionality. For Saleem, the washing basket of invisibility was an ideal place for the observer/voyeur because it was on the periphery of society. Omar occupies just such a space without the necessity for concealment: 'From his position at the edge of the school's life, he took vicarious pleasure in the activities of those around him…' (S, 45). Here he is able to experience the benefits of his own brand of social 'near-invisibility' (S, 45).

Interestingly, the narrator figure makes no bones about the fact that he regards Omar's activities as those of a voyeur. Unlike those of Saleem in *Midnight's Children* and Baal in *The Satanic Verses*, these activities are not complicated by the consideration that the watcher is an artist (Omar is a poet in name only) and therefore possesses licence to observe and to derive a vicarious satisfaction from the activities of others. Omar's experience of 'the infinitely rich and cryptic texture of human life and… the bitter-sweet delights of living through other human beings' (S, 46) is a confession of the illicit pleasures of life experienced at a remove from one's own direct participation in it. By assuming the career of physician, Omar can achieve the ultimate in legitimate voyeurism. Like Aadam Aziz in *Midnight's Children*, sanctioned in his negotiation of the perforated sheet separating him from Naseem, Omar is permitted to probe the secrets of the human body; a figure simultaneously central and peripheral to the mechanics of existence.

The setting for the opening chapters of *Shame* is the border town of Q – a more generalised and anonymous location than the Ellowen Deeowen of *The Satanic Verses*, but which can be identified with Quetta in Pakistan. Geography and topography are as central to the construction and argument of *Shame* as they are to Rushdie's other texts. The narrative voice informs the reader that the text's treatment of Pakistan is a matter of 'off-centring':

> The country in this story is not Pakistan, or not quite. There are two countries, real and fictional, occupying the same space. My story, my fictional country exist, like myself, at a slight angle to reality. (S, 29)

The haphazard nature of the division of India after independence to allow for the formation of Pakistan, and the subsequent secession of Bangladesh, has confronted writers in the sub-continent with the image of a land mass separated by divisions which seem more imagined than concrete. This idea of 'imagined' divisions, which has a long history as a theme in South Asian fiction, is taken up again by the writer Amitav Ghosh in his 1988 novel *The Shadow Lines* where Calcutta and Dhaka seem split only by the ethereal divisions of the title, and in which the narrator states that 'a place does not merely exist, ... it has to be invented in one's imagination.'[11]

These shadow lines, the frontiers that cross the thematic, textual and geographical terrain of *Shame*, are everywhere apparent. There is the boundary line on the frontier patrolled by Farah Zoroaster and her father; the hinterland of 'respectable' society where those who have transgressed against its rules must live out their days. Farah's father turns prophet of doom in the wilderness of the desert, perched naked on a bollard like the hermits of the Middle Ages, talking to the sun and 'begging it to come down to earth and engulf the planet in its brilliant cleansing fire' (*S*, 54). This father/daughter relationship played out on the demarcation line between sin and respectability, is the obverse and mirror of Arjumand and Iskander's life. Arjumand preserves the sanctity of her father and his mission in the world of the Pakistani élite, while Farah and her father eke out an existence on the edges of the nation, of society and of sanity. Designated as 'different' from the outset, a Zoroastrian in Pakistan, looked after by a Goan, Farah, as proven sexual reprobate, inhabits the borderline area, her sexual otherness consigned to the margin which marks out the limits of shame's acceptability.

The horizon is also the place 'out there' where fantasies and dreams settle and take root. Haroun Harappa fixes his sights on the horizon – on the limits of his existence – to focus on his uncle Iskander whose world of power and success seems to lie just beyond it. For Omar Khayyam Shakil there is the fearful border between sleep and waking which is patrolled with a watchful eye on the approach of nightmares and the void beyond, while

Bilquìs Hyder makes a dual journey across the frontiers of sanity and madness, life and death. Omar's own circular trip back to his home, Nishapur, is linked to his terror of the frontier. Though a peripheral man, the world still has an edge to it, a limit over which it is still possible for him to slip into oblivion:

> he ought to know that the border is the edge of his world, the rim of things, and that the real dreams are these far-fetched notions of getting across that supernatural frontier into some wild hallucination of a promised land. (S, 268)

Just how much control this schema exerts over the narrative is illustrated by Rushdie's own remarks on the subject of textual frontiers:

> You know how *Shame* uses ideas of the frontier a lot, the frontier is like a trap, people faint when they get near it and beyond the frontier is the void, and so on? Well, having set up that idea it seemed that the characters had accepted it more than I had, so whenever I got them anywhere near the frontier they would refuse to cross it.[12]

Despite the disingenuousness with which Rushdie abdicates the creative and controlling responsibility for his characters, as he did with Saleem in *Midnight's Children*, his comments highlight the rigidity of the framework imposed on the text by the internal structure of such motifs as the frontier. Having constructed a pattern and a 'point' for the narrative, the two features are forced to coalesce in a way that suffocates the internal movement that was so obvious and defining a feature of *Midnight's Children*.

What then is the effect of the narrator's declaration in the second section of the text that he is not attempting a realistic portrait of Pakistan, but a general discussion of oppressive and repressive social and political regimes? He goes on to outline some of the historical facts that such a realistic novel would deal with, effectively performing the task he claims to avoid. The reason given for side-stepping 'factuality' is that such a work of realism centred on a recognisable society would lead to its being banned and burned, and that he was therefore under an obligation to universalise Pakistan's story in order to get round this. This statement, however, is immediately undercut by the 'list' of subjects he would have had to avoid, thereby providing the accusation of Pakistan's oppressions that he said he was forced to forego. To have made the book any less obviously 'about' Pakistan would have undercut the oft-declared political motivation of Rushdie's writing. Even within the very act of espousing the universalising anti-realist or 'magical realist' form, Rushdie makes an implicit criticism of it: 'I am only telling a sort of modern fairy-tale, so that's all right; nobody need get upset, or take anything I say too seriously. No drastic action need be taken either. What a relief!' (*S*, 70).

This would seem to support the argument returned to in the final section of this study that Rushdie's work abjures the label of magical realism precisely because the latter can induce in its readers a feeling of quietism; a feeling that its arguments – conducted at a remove from political reality – can ultimately be ignored. Magical realism may be the ideal form for representing the fragmented histories of post-colonial societies but it may also, by its lack of specificity, allow its (particularly western) readers to abdicate from any responsibility for changing the realities. The irony with which Rushdie plays on the concept of fairy-tale in his construction of *Shame* is borne out by his treatment of the central 'historical' figures in the text and in the corresponding drama of Pakistani politics. Like the Black Widow of *Midnight's Children* and Mrs Torture of *The Satanic Verses*, 'Virgin Ironpants' and 'Old Razor Guts' are clearly recognisable objects of criticism. The reader is never left in any doubt as to who (individually) or what (socially, culturally, politically) Rushdie is pointing his less-than-subtle satirist's finger at. This is no fairy-tale for children.

As for the narrative techniques employed in *Shame*, despite the much more tightly ordered and concise format, Rushdie still adopts a digressional, storytelling mode as he did in *Midnight's Children*. This tends to take the form of 'asides' from the narrator to illustrate the intersections of Pakistan's story with his own experience, allowing him to insert himself into the narrative as a bit-player. The central story itself is made manifest by a process of alternate concealments and revelations, where a taste of things to come is offered to whet the reader's/audience's appetite before being forced back into its rightful place in the narrative. This digressive technique illustrates both the power of the storyteller in controlling the narrative and his potential as subject of his own discourse. As with the manipulation of leitmotif and digression in *Midnight's Children*, this is evidence of a vice-like authorial control rather than a chaotic assemblage of material.

Timothy Brennan argues that the *Qur'ān* is an important model and intertext for *Shame* and that this has implications for the narrative structure of the text. Certainly the holy book of Islam is invoked many times in *Shame*, whether as the guide to conduct for the new Islamic nation-state or in its more private incarnations as the place where births, deaths and marriages are recorded, while the oft-repeated story of Bilquìs's escape from her father's burning cinema becomes legitimised and solidified through retelling into the one authoritative 'sacred text' (*S*, 76). Sufi mysticism, at the heart of *Grimus* is also recalled when Omar stumbles across a walnut screen among Nishapur's jumbled antiquities, which depicts Qaf mountain and the thirty birds of 'Attar's narrative. In 'the age of Khomeini' (*S*, 241) which has subsequently failed to end for Rushdie, Sufi symbolism seems to point away from the strictures of fundamentalism towards a more individual, even inspirational access to spirituality.

Within the general framework of the narrative, the stories of the individual protagonists assert their right to be told and to leave their imprint on the shape of the collective narrative. *Shame* reinforces Saleem Sinai's declaration in *Midnight's Children* that an individual's sense of personal history is the 'glue of personality'. The women of Bariamma's zenana recount their individual histories to each other, picking out the details of the weave that makes up the complete fabric of the text: 'such stories, were the glue that held the clan together, binding the generations in webs of whispered secrets' (*S*, 76). Each woman's story gains the right to be recounted and heard over time, just as that of the post-colonial subject has forced itself to be heard and given credence.

Alongside these stories are the gaps or holes which help to delineate the pattern of the textual fabric. For every story recounted there are countless untold alternatives. 'All stories', the text informs us, 'are haunted by the ghosts of the stories they might have been' (*S*, 116). It almost reads like the argument of a deconstructionist; that what is missing from the text, its absences, articulate as much if not more than what is present. In the case of *Shame*, the narrative voice worries that the story of 'Peccavistan' is excluding that of 'Proper London', eventually told in *The Satanic Verses*. An alternative angle on the presence/absence dualism is that offered by the 'feminisation' of the 'masculine' plot. The stories of the women's lives which provide the framework for the exploits of the heroes, are seen as the natural obverse of the intended male-centred universe – the '"male" plot refracted, so to speak, through the prisms of its reverse and "female" side' (*S*, 173).

This dualism may not in itself be entirely positive, when one considers that, for example, Bilquìs's story is articulated in the enclosed, 'private' sphere of the women's quarters, and Rani Harappa's embroidered narrative of her husband's vices remains hidden in a trunk, only ever viewed by the resentful eyes of her daughter. This public/private separation inevitably undermines the authority of the women's stories.

The fascination/obsession with the domestic and sexual power of women which is always present in Rushdie's work, is more evident in *Shame* than anywhere else. The text's declared project to voice the silenced stories of Pakistan's oppressed women is often admired by critics without consideration of the way it is undercut by the representation of the women themselves. Anuradha Dingwaney Needham, for example, celebrates 'the complex ways in which *women* and their *histories* are recovered and inserted into the "alternate" history of Pakistan'.[13] Timothy Brennan states that Rushdie 'weaves into the fabric of *Shame* that most Western of political challenges, feminism'[14] while it can even be argued that Rushdie invokes the iconic feminist victim – the 'madwoman in the attic' – when he depicts the slumbering, sedated and bestial Sufiya Zinobia imprisoned in the family home by her menfolk.

But Omar's resentment of his peripheral position in relation to his mothers serves as yet another instance of the blend of confusion, frustration and even outright hostility towards the relative autonomy of women which surfaces in Rushdie's fiction. Rape often bursts through as the ultimate signification of this resentment – Flapping Eagle's rape of the goddess Axona, for example, and in *Shame*, Omar's assault on the hypnotised Farah Zoroaster. Sexuality is explored and exploited by rendering the woman in the equation effectively powerless. Omar's resentment of his mothers' closeness has a further edge of unpleasantness to it when viewed alongside other instances of such resentments:

> he hated them for their closeness, for the way they sat with arms entwined on their swinging, creaking seat, for their tendency to lapse giggling into the private language of their girlhood. (S, 35)

One is reminded of the mood of this confrontation in *The Satanic Verses* when Saladin takes an instant dislike to the 'self-contained… essence' of Allie Cone (*SV*, 428). The suggestion is offered to us that Omar is effectively taking revenge on his mothers in all his subsequent dealings with women. This impulse is highlighted in a reference to the shared debaucheries of Omar and Iskander. Here, Omar's ability to hypnotise women for sexual purposes – an extreme representation of male manipulation of women – is undercut by the ambivalence of the narrative voice. The objects of Omar's attentions are merely 'white women of a certain type' who possess 'admittedly scanty inhibitions' (S, 128); the perversity of their semi-rape undermined by the narrator's value-judgements on women.

Rushdie's treatment of the sisters' 'arrested sexuality' (S, 13) depicts them as sexually naive, but this is counterbalanced by the prurience with which the narrative voice ponders on the nature of the sisters' solidarity. This bond, it is suggested, may have been sealed in menstrual blood – a seal representative in itself of secrecy, otherness and a vague menace. We are told that the sisters inhabit their father, Old Shakil's 'labyrinthine' (S, 13) mansion and, as in *The Satanic Verses*, this concept of the labyrinth seems somehow feminised. Just as the whores of 'The Curtain' wait at the centre of their labyrinthine brothel and protect Baal in the *The Satanic Verses*, so the Shakil sisters, once their collective pregnancy becomes known, withdraw into the secret corners of their own labyrinth, sealing themselves off from the penetrating gaze and prying curiosity of the outside world. The stiletto blades that lurk lethally inside the dumbwaiter – the only means of access into their protected stronghold – come to represent what we are made to regard as the twisted sexuality of the sisters; a vagina dentata, something destructive rather than creative. They become a direct image of the threat posed by female sexuality which seems to lie behind so many of Rushdie's characterisations of women. Should man succeed in penetrating the defences a woman constructs around her, there might still be a surprise in store for him, waiting to destroy him.

Nishapur, the Shakil home, is also a labyrinth for the young Omar Khayyam Shakil; an 'underlit corridory edifice' (*S*, 30). It is presented as a limbo world between real and unreal, material and spiritual. The woman-centred claustrophobia of Nishapur is presented as a womb to which Omar seeks to cling. The decaying bowels of the house become like a parallel universe of faded antiquity to set beside the real world outside. Omar's accidental glimpse of this outside world through a crumbling wall strikes immediate fear into him and sends him running back indoors – back to the womb – rather than risk venturing forth. It is an image that also finds a reflection in one of Fitzgerald's translated quatrains from Umar Khayyam:

> Myself when young did eagerly frequent
> Doctor and Saint, and heard great argument
> About it and about, but evermore
> Came out by the same door where in I went.[15]

That Rushdie slips into such a clichéd use of a womb image to represent Omar's home, illustrates both the structural imperatives imposed on the text by its desire for circularity, and also, once more, the idea that a female refuge from the dangers of the outside world would represent a threat as well as a haven. The 'womb' of Nishapur serves more as a revelation (albeit involuntary) of Rushdie's psychology than an interesting elaboration of the narrative.

How far then is Rushdie guilty of self-deception in his apparent belief in himself as a champion of women? It is certainly true that considerable narrative time is given over to female characters in *Shame* as it is in his other texts, and that this does serve in many respects to point up and humanise the stories of his heroes. But this formal manoeuvre and superficial even-handedness finds itself time and again in conflict with other forces, presumably stemming from the same culture – and gender-based prejudices and conditioning which Rushdie purports to explode. In Chapter Seven of the text, the narrative voice intervenes to declare its understanding of the Muslim fathers who feel compelled to murder their 'shameless' westernised daughters. Rushdie imagines just such a daughter whom he calls Anahita Muhammed: 'She danced behind my eyes, her nature changing each time I glimpsed her: now innocent, now whore, then a third and a fourth thing. But finally she eluded me' (*S*, 116).

It is an image he returns to in *The Satanic Verses* where the 'Anahita' of Anahita Muhammed and the 'Sufiya' of Sufiya Zinobia are taken up again to create the two worldly Asian sisters, Anahita and Mishal Sufiyan who live at the Shaandaar Café. The way in which Anahita is imagined in *Shame*, 'now innocent, now whore', cuts deep to a culturally-conditioned belief that will not allow him to conceive of women except in extreme terms. It also exposes his sense of frustration at being unable to control this image – unable ultimately to *bid* a woman to be one thing or another. The innocent/whore binarism extends beyond the actual women who appear in the text to embrace abstractions and inanimate objects. Karachi itself is shown to age from 'slender girlish town' to 'obese harridan' – a 'painted lady' of 'overblown charms.' (*S*, 118). Bilquìs's father Mahmoud comments on the emotions and images that attach to the word 'Woman': 'Is there no end to the burdens this word is capable of bearing? Was there ever such a broad-backed and also such a dirty word?' (*S*, 62).

Therein lies the root of both the innocent/whore and shame/shamelessness binarisms in the text – that the concept of Woman like women themselves can embody both sides of each of these coins. In societal terms, it is the understanding that, for example, great sexual repression and extremes of uninhibited and unconstrained sexual activity can not only occur within the same society but are interdependent; equal and opposite forces, with repression fanning the flame of abandon. Even Sufiya Zinobia herself – the embodiment of the desire for revenge against the nation's collective shame – also serves as the ultimate manifestation of the destructive capabilities of female sexuality. Destroying those who seek sexual union with her, she becomes as much like the black widow spider as she does Nemesis – indeed, an amalgam of the black *burqa* of shame and oppression and the 'shameless' autocracy of the 'black widow' Indira Gandhi as we see her in *Midnight's Children*.

Aijaz Ahmad sees Sufiya becoming 'the oldest of the misogynist myths: the virgin who is really a vampire, the irresistible temptress who seduces men in order to kill them.'[16] Even the too-perfect Muslim daughter, Arjumand Harappa, becomes one of a number of Rushdie's characters whose obsessive love refuses to recognise the taboos of kinship. Her near-identification with Iskander as lover – rejecting the needs of her body to punish it into becoming the repository of his memory – mirrors Saleem Sinai's incestuous love for Jamila Singer, Flapping Eagle's sexual relationship with his sister Bird-Dog in *Grimus* and the cloying closeness of Gibreel Farishta and his mother in *The Satanic Verses*. As Ahmad again says, 'the frustration of erotic need, which drives some to frenzy and others to nullity, appears in every case to be the central fact of a woman's existence'.[17]

If Rushdie fails in successfully articulating a female narrative of Pakistan's history, it is nevertheless true that it is in *Shame* that a coherent and positive image of the migrant postcolonial subject is projected. Both the real and fictional Pakistans were born out of the experience of migration – the mass migrations, particularly in the Punjab, following the partition of India in 1947, which led to the splitting of Rushdie's own family. The concept of migration for Rushdie builds in layers upon that initial movement of peoples, the historic migration of the prophet Mohammed's followers – the *mohajirs* – out of Mecca and into Medina during their early persecution. Migration, flight and dislocation are perpetual themes in Rushdie's writing and the means by which he seeks to express the peculiar sensibility of the migrant writer as it searches for new forms, new techniques, new worlds in which it can define itself. Musing on the unlocatable dystopia of Terry Gilliam's film *Brazil*, Rushdie writes of the migrant as one who is rooted in ideas and memories rather than places and material objects and who has a profound mistrust of what constitutes 'reality' (*IH*, 125).

The narrator of *Shame* provides a long digression on the relationship between migration, flight and gravity:

> I have a theory that the resentments we *mohajirs* engender have something to do with our conquest of the force of gravity. We have performed the act of which all men anciently dream, the thing for which they envy the birds; that is to say, we have flown. (S, 85)

Gravity, for Rushdie, is the physical force that corresponds to the more abstract notion of 'belonging'. To oppose gravity is to be like the migrant, to engage in 'flight'. *Mohajir* or migrant is a title and identity Rushdie continues to employ for all the uprooted and displaced characters who people his texts. In *Shame* the narrative voice declares 'I… am a translated man. I have been borne across. It is generally believed that something is always lost in translation. I cling to the notion … that something can also be gained' (S, 29). In terms of the Omar/Umar parallel, Umar's poetry now exists for us in a translated, mediated form, far removed from its original incarnation but nonetheless possessing its own character and charm.

The idea of translation as a metaphor for the migrant's condition was expanded in a conversation between Rushdie and the German writer Günter Grass in the British Channel Four television series *Voices*. Rushdie says – 'I discovered that if you look etymologically at the meaning of the word metaphor and the word translation… it turned out they meant the same thing. See, translation from the Latin means to carry across. Metaphor from the Greek means to carry across… this comes back to my pre-occupation with the idea of migration. People are also carried across.'[18] What is important for Rushdie's growing embrace of hybridity and the positive aspects of being borne across frontiers is that, as Anuradha Dingwaney Needham puts it, 'for Rushdie, as for the narrator of *Shame*, habitation on borders… is "not infertile"'[19] Translation is again alluded to in *The Satanic Verses* as one of the processes by which something new is formed, while the flight of migrants is taken beyond the idea introduced in *Shame* to become a central metaphor of the later text.

Part of *Shame*'s concern with migration and belonging, centres on the loneliness of internal exile for those out of political favour, the exile of Farah Zoroaster and Eduardo Rodrigues to atone for her sexual 'indiscretion' and the act of destruction which forces Bilquìs out of her old world and into a new one. Though Bilquìs adjusts admirably to the role of Mrs Raza Hyder at first, her own increasing sense of dislocation, brought about in part by her fail-ure to 'locate' herself firmly in the role of good Muslim wife by producing sons, is figured in her paranoid fear of the Loo wind. Although she ceases to have any contact with it, she still clings desperately to her furniture and possessions, longing for fixity in a world that threatens her with dispersal and disarray.

One thing the migrant can try to use to locate him or herself after migration is possessions. To lose them, leave them behind or abjure their influence is to threaten oneself with dislocation, loss of 'belonging'. Farah and Eduardo are unsentimental about possessions; resigned to the idea that through cultural difference and sexual transgression, they do not 'belong' in Q. Omar Khayyam Shakil's way of destroying the tyranny of Nishapur and its suffocating history is to literally destroy the artefacts which represent it. The tears he sheds at this act of wanton van-dalism, register his own implicit understanding of the loss at the very moment that he wills it.

Unlike Saleem Sinai's globe and Saladin Chamcha's lamp, the broken artefacts do not register a cherished connection with the past but are merely 'the corpses of [Omar's] useless massacred history' (*S*, 32). This is perhaps one of the reasons why belongings and 'belonging' are treated somewhat differently in *Shame* than in Rushdie's other texts. As Pakistanis, the history of Farah, Bilquìs and Omar is necessarily one that incorporates massacre and division. Those objects which come to represent it therefore speak of a past which is painful rather than affirmative. Old Shakil's purchase of a British library in its entirety symbolises the less painful option of a surface borrowing from other cultures, like the symbolic takeover of the intact Englishness of the Methwold Estate in *Midnight's Children*. It is a bastardisation, rather than an attempt to assert that one's own past was more than a record of disruption and destruction.

Iskander Harappa's attitude to history is similarly informed by an impulse towards social Darwinism; a rejection of maudlin nostalgia in favour of progress: 'History is natural selection. Mutant versions of the past struggle for dominance, new species of fact arise, and old, saurian truths go to the wall, blind-folded and smoking last cigarettes. Only the mutations of the strong survive' (*S*, 124).

It would seem however that Rushdie's own attitude to this stance is that a distinction can be made between the negative connotations of mutation and the positive ones of hybridity. The image of a continuum between cultural 'purity' at the one extreme and hybridity at the other can help to illustrate this. 'Cultural purity' embodies essentialist ideas of what constitutes a particular cultural identity. This identity is seen as clear, because undivided. At the other extreme is hybridity, suggesting an amalgam of different strands and components of cultural identity. Mutation would then lie somewhere between the two while hybridity would be the achievement of a positive blend of elements.

The extent to which *Shame* can be embraced as a truly hybrid novel in terms of its form as well as its content is, however, problematised by its relation to allegorical forms of writing and the suggestion that this leads to the creation of less sophisticated portraits of the post-colonial condition. Of all Rushdie's texts, *Shame* is the one which is most accommodating to this particular categorisation of its form. The text's shifts between reality/unreality; Pakistan/'Peccavistan'; fiction and 'factual' narrative interventions, point up the strong representational or allegorical function of the narrative. If we accept Saleem Sinai's argument that India could not exist except by virtue of an enormous act of collective imagining, then it may be that Rushdie felt 'moth-eaten' Pakistan, 'a country so improbable that it could almost exist' (*S*, 31), would seem to require the sturdier, if rather heavy-handed delineation offered by an allegorical framework, for it to be fully realised. It is as if a series of directly transferable correspondences between people, places and politics helps to shore up the idea of a nation.

The passage which describes Rani Harappa's shawls, depicting the excesses of her husband Iskander's political rule, is the embodiment of the text's movement towards allegorical forms to represent its arguments. Each shawl becomes progressively more allegorical, from the more straightforward 'realist' depictions of Iskander's sexual indiscretions with his white concubines, through the various Machiavellian faces of power – espionage, corruption, electoral abuse, physical repression and torture. With Rani's thirteenth shawl, Iskander is shown with his hands literally round the throat of Democracy, strangling the life out of it. Rani herself becomes Mohenjo, an exiled woman whose very being merges with the elements of the house and the landscape that effectively imprison her.

The last of the eighteen shawls depicts a seeming paradise – Mohenjo as the incarnation of all the ideals on which the 'land of the pure' was conceived – but contaminated centrally and fundamentally by murder. In this instance it is the murder of 'Little' Mir Harappa, but essentially, allegorically, the paradise is contaminated by the sum of all the murders, abuses and corruptions sanctioned by Iskander. The act of collective will that was needed to imagine India into existence in *Midnight's Children* is perverted in *Shame* by the contradictory and conflicting forces of the *individual* wills of such men as Hyder and Harappa. Indeed, Pakistan was itself the creation of the individual wills of such figures as Mohammed Ali Jinnah, the country's first president.

Instead, the collective forces responsible for dreaming the nation into existence become channelled into the 'creation' and motivation of Sufiya, the Beast – 'the collective fantasy of a stifled people' (S, 263), destroying shamelessness in her apocalyptic fury.

But what exactly is the role of allegory in the text as a whole? Is it sufficient to brand *Shame* a 'national allegory' along with the rest of so-called third-world literature as Fredric Jameson does.[20] Timothy Brennan refers us to Aijaz Ahmad's reply to Jameson's influential if over-stated argument, in which Ahmad criticises this generalising slant along with the 'epistemological impossibility'[21] of classifying literature as third-world and the 'empirically ungrounded'[22] nature of Jameson's binary opposition between a capitalist first-world and a pre- or non-capitalist third world. For Ahmad, the predominantly Eurocentric viewpoint of American theorists blinds them to any 'third-world' literature not written in English, allowing them to valorise the work of a writer such as Rushdie for offering a 'voice' to what appears to them to be the otherwise intellectually silenced hordes of the subcontinent. Similarly, the complexities of a Rushdie text which Ahmad sees arising out of his involvement with modernism and postmodernism could not be farther from the allegedly naïve realist impulses of third-world fiction for which Jameson seeks to act as apologist.

But Brennan too, while rejecting the sweep of Jameson's generalisations, nevertheless refers repeatedly in his study of Rushdie's writing to the latter's mode of allegorising in his texts. *Grimus* is 'uninterpretable allegory'; *Midnight's Children* provides an 'allegory of narrative composition'; *Shame* 'allegorically describ[es] the decline in Western dominance as a crisis in European art' while he sees in *The Satanic Verses* 'another allegorical level – the scientific', where 'the immigrant is contending with the barbarous survival strategies of 'natural selection'.[23] This would suggest a general acceptance that Rushdie's writing, despite its theoretical and linguistic complexities, is nevertheless tuned into another literary form – namely allegory – specifically employed to convey the social/political/national arguments of its producer.

What seems singularly lacking in the arguments and counter-arguments around the notion of 'national allegory' is any clear or even approximate definition of what exactly is meant by the term allegory. Jameson, for all the open-handedness with which he applies it to third-world literature, offers us little in the way of concrete categorisation of this genre. For the reader to whom allegory traditionally conjures up the image of Bunyan's *Pilgrim's Progress,* Jameson offers the elusive redefinition of the 'allegorical spirit' as one that is 'profoundly discontinuous, a matter of breaks and heterogeneities, of the multiple polysemia of the dream rather than the homogeneous representation of the symbol'.[24] In relation to third-world literature, the chief characteristic of this, its own brand of allegory, is that 'the story of the private individual destiny is always an allegory of the embattled situation of the public third-world culture and society'.[25] Jameson's generic label – its questionable generalisations aside – cannot account for writing which, like Rushdie's, speaks of the fragmentation of history and identity.

A more recognisable definition of the genre is offered by Gay Clifford in *The Transformations of Allegory* where she isolates its main features as 'the extended... use of personification and personified abstractions and... the incorporation of commentary and interpretation into the action'.[26] Clearly Rushdie's interventions in the text serve to point up and universalise the particular problem of oppression in Pakistan, while Jameson, too, declares that 'authorial intervention, no longer tolerable in realistic narrative, is still perfectly suitable to the allegorical fable as a form'.[27]

But Clifford also, as the title of her study suggests, regards transformation as a recurrent theme of allegory, where a writer embodies his or her belief in the ability of readers to transform themselves by witnessing such a transformation in the central characters of allegorical texts. Does Rushdie, then, believe that his readers 'can be changed and made wiser by the meaning of his work'?[28] Does his continued espousal of political motives in his writing necessarily mean that he believes in the transformative powers of literature? It may be so, without it being the case that *Shame* effects such a transformation.

In one sense, the only transformative novels in Rushdie's œuvre are *The Satanic Verses* and *Haroun and the Sea of Stories* where change, for individuals at least, *is* brought about. *Haroun*, with its employment of the stock allegorical motifs of the quest and of direct correspondences between characters and abstractions, is the most deeply allegorical. Along with *The Satanic Verses*, it demonstrates allegory's transformative powers in a way that his earlier texts do not. Nemesis and/or apocalypse are transformative in a wholly negative sense, in the way that death 'transforms' life without offering anything in its place. Clifford's line of argument goes on to suggest that modern allegories have become increasingly satirical and negative, which could be applied to *Grimus*, *Midnight's Children* and *Shame*, in particular the 'no place'/Utopia of *Grimus*. Also if we follow her example of Orwell's *Animal Farm* as an allegory which asks us to link Napoleon to Stalin at the same time as allowing us to see him as the type of *all* dictators[29] then we can establish a link with Rushdie's repeated claim that Hyder and Harappa both are and are not Zia and Bhutto, at the same time as being the archetypes of dictators the world over.

But is all this still too tenuous to allow us to regard *Shame* in any definitive sense as allegory, national or otherwise? In a 1985 interview, Rushdie resisted the claim that *Shame* was indeed allegory: 'Allegory asks readers to make a translation, to uncover a secret text that has not actually been written. In that sense I don't think my books operate as allegories. I like to think of them as realistic novels myself.'[30]

A solution to the confusion generated by the text can perhaps be seen to lie, as always, in the acceptance of Rushdie's writing as occupying a midway, hybridised point between two polarities of writing – between the symbolism of modernism and postmodernism and the traditional view of allegory with its directly transferable correspondences. It is nearer to the reality of Rushdie's writing to speak of an allegorical *instinct* in his work, modified by his own grounding in and affinities with symbolist literature. Thus Sufiya can simultaneously embody Pakistan's shame while still serving as an image of that nation's potentially apocalyptic nuclear capabilities when she explodes at the end. Such an allegorical instinct can be located in Rushdie's depiction of General Zia in a piece written after the dictator's death:

> Eleven years ago he burst out of his bottle like an *Arabian Nights* goblin, and although he seemed, at first, a small, puny sort of demon, he instantly commenced to grow, until he was gigantic enough to be able to grab the whole of Pakistan by the throat. (*IH*, 53)

It is the self-same image as that of Iskander, picked out in Rani Harappa's matchless embroidery with his hands round the throat of Democracy. Democracy or Pakistan become personified; allegorised, while the perpetrators of these crimes against the nation maintain their 'realistic' proportions. In the same year as the interview in which he rejected the label of allegory for *Shame*, he offered another image of this blending and hybridising technique: 'what I hoped for is that one would make figures in the book who were somehow bigger than the particular instances of them that history had offered us'.[31]

Rushdie's technique in *Shame* therefore becomes a way of playing with reality, with real figures and national entities that puts them, as he says of his fictional Pakistan and of himself, 'at a slight angle to reality'. A discussion of the migrant's cultural and historical situation attempts to force its way out of the closed circle of the text, but *Shame* was the arena for Rushdie to display his political credentials rather than his skill at depicting that situation. Like *Grimus*, it hints at the necessary next stage of development in Rushdie's writing, towards the expansion of the idea of migration as flight and the rejection of mutation in favour of hybridity.

The Satanic Verses

IT was in seeking to answer the question posed at the beginning of this study – 'How does newness come into the world?' – that Rushdie came to find himself, like so many of his heroes, a truly peripheral man. Pushed literally to the edges of society, into its most secret spaces, a terrible unmaking of his own identity has been occasioned. His name now conjures up not just images of an affronted and enraged religious force,[1] but also for Britain's own white majority, an image of a fanatical, book-burning section of its own population, an apparent fulfilment of Enoch Powell's prophecies of the chaos that attaches to unassimilable difference. Whether as the face on an imaginary 'WANTED!' poster, or as the object of the liberal intelligentsia's genteel disdain,[2] his identity, his work and his ideas are as open to re- and misinterpretation as the lives and actions of earlier colonial subjects. 'Salman Rushdie' is what Islam, critics, the media and the general public say he is.

It is as much the tragedy of the text as of its author that *The Satanic Verses* became a byword for trouble – trouble within and between cultures, religions, different sections of society. Since its publication in 1988, the text has all but lost its ability to be judged as an artistic enterprise rather than a cultural and political crisis. Discussions of its qualities and merits are lost in the welter of debates that variously locate themselves around, behind and beyond the so-called 'Rushdie affair'. A refusal to discuss the text as an exploration of the condition of the migrant, post-colonial subject, fails to recognise that the dynamism of the novel resides in its handling of the issues that have developed in importance in Rushdie's work – the relationships between location and dislocation, past and present, memory and history.

Rushdie's controversial treatment of events within the life of the prophet Mohammed allows him to deal with his different agendas through a comparison with a particular historical situation, namely the founding of Islam. Accounts of the prophet's life detail his experience of visions even in early childhood and it was *c*.AD 610 that he was called upon to recite the word of Allah while in retreat on Mount Hira. Mohammed's vision of the angel Gabriel/Gibreel delivering to him the message of the *Qur'ān*, holds within it the problem of distinguishing whether such voices come from within or outside the individual. One man's prophet is another man's schizo and indeed Maxime Rodinson in his study of the prophet speaks of 'a certain pathological element in his make-up'.[3]

The incident of the satanic verses themselves, around which the text is structured, is accepted by some scholars and contested by others. The scholar and translator of the *Qur'ān*, N. J. Dawood, describes the accepted pre-history of Islam thus:

> Long before Muhammad's call, Arabian paganism was showing signs of decay. At the Ka'bah the Meccans worshipped not only Allah, the supreme Semitic God, but also a number of female deities whom they regarded as the daughters of Allah. Among these were Al-Lat, Al-Uzza, and Manat, who represented the Sun, Venus, and Fortune respectively.[4]

In *The Satanic Verses*, Uzza, we are told, represents beauty and love; Manat, Fate; while Lat is the omnipotent mother-goddess, Allah's female counterpart (*SV*, 99–100). The point of contention among scholars of the *Qur'ān* is whether verses were inserted into the holy book in the early days of Islam, in order to placate the polytheistic peoples of Mecca and bring about greater tolerance of the new religion. Rodinson sees this as an example of Mohammed's 'unconscious suggesting to him a formula which provided a practical road to unanimity'.[5] The Islamic source al-Tabari states that Mohammed received the verses praising the intercession of the goddesses but that these were removed from the *Qur'ān* when Gibreel informed the Prophet that they were verses inspired by the devil.[6] The recitation and subsequent rescinding of the verses are separated by just ten pages in *The Satanic Verses*. 'Mahound', the dream-prophet of the text whose title is the medieval demonisation of the real prophet's name, is offered tolerance of his new religion in return for acceptance of the goddesses. He provides it: 'Have you thought upon Lat and Uzza, and Manat, the third, the other? … They are the exalted birds, and their intercession is desired indeed' (*SV*, 114).

That the goddesses were a significant obstacle to Islam's development is clear from the fact that they still appear in the *Qur'ān* itself. Within the text of Dawood's translation of the holy book, there is reference to the pagan triumvirate, in surah 53:20–26 entitled 'The Star':

> Have you thought on Al-Lat and Al-Uzza and on
> Manat, the third other? Are you to have the
> sons and He the daughters? This is indeed an
> unfair distinction! They are but names which
> you and your fathers have invented: God has
> vested no authority in them.[7]

Part of the significance of these verses to Rushdie's text is their central debate about the importance and power of women. *The Satanic Verses* does not set itself up as a project to espouse the cause of women in the same way as *Shame*, but it quite deliberately hinges the course of events in the text on the actions and interventions of its many female characters. The importance of the women to the central theme of reconstructing migrant identity will be returned to later.

Saladin Chamcha and Gibreel Farishta, the free-falling protagonists of *The Satanic Verses*, provide the most direct image in Rushdie's fiction of the post-colonial subject in collision with his world. Their descent on England, the 'fabled country of Vilayet' (*SV*, 35)[8] from the wreckage of a hijacked aircraft, is replete with the tensions of their condition – on the one hand, defying the laws of gravity, on the other, 'just two brown men, falling hard, nothing so new about that you may think' (*SV*, 5). This fall encapsulates the process of transmutation, or translation as described in *Shame*, whereby the migrant's identity is transformed through the very act of migration. Gibreel, famed for his halitosis, is granted full movie-star perfection, while Saladin receives the gift of foul breath along with that of sprouting horns as he begins to assume demonic characteristics. Here the flight, the journey downwards to earth, illustrates the active processes of change that take place in the migrant as he moves between cultures.

The discussion of *Shame* posited the idea of mutation existing on a continuum between the extremes of cultural purity and hybridity. Saladin, as he sits on the aeroplane prior to the explosion, seeks a typically English form of cultural identity which slips from him like a mask. Hybridity is the end of his journey, while mutation, physical and metaphorical, is the tumultuous process he must pass through *en route*. The zone in which the changes to the two men occur is 'illusory, discontinuous, metamorphic' (*SV*, 5). It is an arena of transformation and translation but one which, through the idea of discontinuity, introduces a jarring note into this process of change. The struggle with discontinuity of identity takes place within a twilight zone for both men. Their identities, their selves, are at this point porous and vulnerable, open to both positive and negative possibilites of transformation – 'there was a fluidity, an indistinctness, at the edges of them' (*SV*, 8).

The extent to which Rushdie has achieved a positive reassertion of the migrant's identity in *The Satanic Verses* can be judged in part by a comparison of the text with V. S. Naipaul's *The Enigma of Arrival*[9] published the previous year. Similar issues of location and dislocation, of the reintegration of the past into the present are examined by both writers. Similar images and scenarios are presented in both, but the conclusions reached and the sentiments evoked differ widely.

Both *The Satanic Verses* and *The Enigma of Arrival* illustrate the migrant's problems of self-contextualisation – of being both located and dislocated, having to orient himself to his new surroundings and of feeling alienated from them, as well as from aspects of his own history and identity. The shifts that have taken place in the settings of Rushdie's texts themselves, from the unlocatable geography of *Grimus*, through India where he was born, Pakistan to which his family moved after partition, and now England, reflect the need to explore the effects of migration and dislocation through to the point where they become manifest in the internalised disorder of divided personalities. The specific topography of *The Satanic Verses* also suggests a greater commitment on Rushdie's part to his arguments about migration. The Vilayet of *The Satanic Verses* moves away from the curious paralleling of *Shame*. With its capital, the mysterious Ellowen Deeowen, it is both imaginative territory and geographical reality – both the arena onto which the fantasies of the migrant are projected and the harsh reality which confronts them when they literally come down to earth.

The imaginary, fantasised nature of Vilayet, the migrant's preconceptions about his new home and the identity he invents to coincide with those preconceptions, are concerns of both *The Satanic Verses* and Naipaul's *Enigma*. For Naipaul, this reinvention of identity leads to the process of mimicry that he describes in *An Area of Darkness* and which recollects the 'imagined' Indias of Forster and Scott mentioned earlier. He states that it 'is a mimicry not of England, a real country, but of the fairy-tale land of Anglo-India'.[10] For Rushdie, the two are not so easily separated – the real and the imagined, England and Vilayet, fade in and out of each other.

Saladin and Gibreel are both actors, both adept at mimicry of one kind or another; cultural chameleons. Saladin's personality, we are told, is 'a half-reconstructed affair of mimicry and voices' (*SV*, 9). With his female counterpart Mimi Mamoulian, he monopolises the market for advertising voice-overs; creating multiple unrealities of identity for commercial exploitation. To his Indian lover, Zeeny Vakil, his personality is like a palimpsest; a slate wiped clean of its Indianness and reinscribed by Anglophilia. Gibreel's identity as star of the Bombay talkies seems equally an affair of temporary and transient construction, as figured in the decaying images of him on street hoardings. His speedy disintegration after disappearing from the set of his latest film is likened to the death of God – the failure of an image to continue to inspire belief in its existence. Like the text itself, Gibreel's identity within and outside his films, breaches the interfaces between fantasy and reality, mortal and deity, sacred and profane. Nicholas D. Rombes Jr. in '*The Satanic Verses* as Cinematic Narrative', sees Rushdie as deliberately exploring 'the modern spectacle of religion and its cinematization',[11] while the novel as a whole is imbued with a cinematic vocabulary which plays on 'ways of seeing' and the flattened reality of modernity, 'expos[ing] the camera's potential shortcomings via the very language and structure of cinema itself.'[12]

The label of *mohajir* or migrant, rehearsed in *Shame*, cannot be applied to Gibreel in the same way as it can to Saladin. Saladin has fulfilled his desire to leave India, to make the journey from Indianness to Englishness, while Gibreel is making the trip in order to pursue the mountain climber Allie Cone with whom he is infatuated. But Gibreel's acting career in the theologicals, personifying the various avatars of the Hindu pantheon, has seen him employed to perform constant reinventions of identity. His very name, like Saladin's, is reinvented. Name-changing and its consequences is a fundamental trope of post-colonial writing: Bharati Mukherjee's Jasmine becomes both Jyoti and Jane as her environment dictates,[13] while in Toni Morrison's writing, black Americans seek the names that have been taken from them in their servitude. The relinquishing and reacceptance of names as the index to identity is as crucial to such texts as it is to all of Rushdie's fictions. Saladin, who was Salahuddin and will be once again, is able to consolidate the diffuse elements of his identity by the end of the text. Gibreel, who was Ismail but who is forever alienated and disconnected from that former self, remains incapable of drawing together his shattered, schizophrenic personality. His adopted persona has been that of the fulfiller of dreams, first the dream of his mother that he should be an angel – a *farishta* – then the dreams of thousands of cinema-goers.

Gibreel's perspective on reality is unlike that of the migrant Naipaul in his Wiltshire cottage. In *The Enigma of Arrival*, Naipaul's hold on this English reality is obscured by his perception of the insipidity and regularity of his surroundings; the incessant rain outside his window which mirrors the blankness of his own gaze. Gibreel, in contrast, is able to see below the iceberg surface of reality to the nine-tenths beneath. He has a confirmed belief in the supernatural, while Naipaul seems to exhibit contempt for fantasy and anti-realism. The reality which eventually becomes so clear to Naipaul that he feels he understands it fully, is, for Gibreel, 'dense' and 'blinding' (*SV*, 22).

Naipaul makes an early distinction in the text between England and 'the tropical street where I had grown up' (*The Enigma of Arrival*, 11). The new land is not invested with any meaning for him. It only acquires this through a corresponding drainage of meaning from his memories of his past in Trinidad. Things seemed blurred and indistinct. Naipaul's narrative presents the paradox of a clear vision which is nevertheless unable to see clearly. It is the migrant's dilemma of being unable to contextualise himself; to find a framework in which he can see his relation to the world. It is the fragmentation and disintegration of identity which arises from the strangeness and unfamiliarity of a new location. For both Naipaul and for Saladin Chamcha in *The Satanic Verses*, the initial process of location that we witness is achieved through the relation to the image of the coloniser. Naipaul finds a space for himself in an image of Salisbury recollected from a print of Constable's painting of the cathedral, on a wall back home in Trinidad.

Naipaul's commentary on his surroundings in Wiltshire – the landscape, the old farm buildings – makes clear the distinctions the narrative sets up between past and present. It is not the presence of the past which Rushdie's writing attempts to evoke as a living, continuing thing, helping to shape the migrant's identity. Naipaul's narrative chronicles the dereliction of parts of history both for himself and for the English rural community he lives among. Here the past is merely preserved for its antique value; it is effectively dead. It mirrors a similar dereliction through dissociation in Naipaul himself: 'That idea of ruin and dereliction, of out-of-placeness, was something I felt about myself' (*Enigma*, 19). It is the same sense of disorientation experienced by Gibreel in London as he wanders its streets with his *A–Z*.

Both narratives share the sense of being informed by the writer's sense of their own mortality. It pervades *The Enigma of Arrival*, which contains an account of the death of Naipaul's sister and is dedicated to the memory of his brother. Death, for Naipaul, highlights processes of change and decay. For Rushdie in *The Satanic Verses*, it seems more positive, providing closure for the unfinalised Saladin, a sense of realness. The death of his father Changez draws together past and present for Saladin, re-affirming the validity of Saleem Sinai's declaration in *Midnight's Children* that 'what you were is forever who you are' (*MC*, 368). For Naipaul, the outlook is bleaker – 'Change was constant. People died. People grew old' (*Enigma*, 34).

The discomfiture experienced by Naipaul on arriving in England is often figured through associations with food, as it is with Saladin. Naipaul speaks of the secrecy and embarrassment with which he attempts to consume the food of his own culture he has been given for the journey; the bananas which ripen drastically on the flight to London and the roasted chicken provided to spare his Brahmin sensitivities from the contamination of others' hands (*Enigma*, 105). Saladin's first trip to England with his father is crucial for establishing the alienation between them. Forced to look after the expenses of their trip, in other words to take responsibility for his decision to become Anglicised, Saladin feels unable to allow himself proper meals and he too is forced to consume a roasted chicken secretly in his room:

> Chicken-breasted beneath the gaze of dowagers and liftwallahs he felt the birth of that implacable rage which would burn within him for over a quarter of a century… which would fuel perhaps his determination to become the thing that his father was-not-could-never-be, that is a goodandproper Englishman. (*SV*, 43)

Later, at public school in England, Saladin experiences his confrontation with the indigestible kipper of British social customs (*SV*, 44). His father's ability to buy him a place in society does not guarantee a corresponding acceptance from those around him, or indeed his own ability to swallow on the kipper. Naipaul was embarrassed by his association with the food of his old culture, while Saladin struggles with the bones of the new.

Memory plays a crucial part in Rushdie's writing as the force which shapes the migrant's sense of history. Memory for Naipaul is, in part, that which allows him his passport to Englishness; his ability to memorise facts and figures in school in order to pass the necessary examinations to get into Oxford. His description of this process is interesting in its relation to the disorientation of the migrant and the way this also comes to be figured in *The Satanic Verses*. He writes: 'So much of my education had been... abstract, a test of memory: like a man, denied the chance of visiting famous cities, learning their street maps instead' (*Enigma*, 108). The *A–Z* of London streets becomes the migrant's key to the labyrinthine secrets of the city for Gibreel in *The Satanic Verses*.[14] Naipaul says of his experience of the city that he 'was used to living in a world where the signs were without meaning, or without the meaning intended by their makers' (*Enigma*, 120). In London he becomes 'like a man trying to get to know a city from its street map alone' (*Enigma*, 121).

The process of 'translation' to England for Naipaul brings about a division. 'I could feel the two sides of myself separating one from the other, the man from the writer' (*Enigma*, 111). Writing, for Naipaul, is the assumption of an identity that is other to himself rather than an amalgam of experience. Until the publication of *The Enigma of Arrival*, his fictional career had largely been the record of narratives of colonial experience which had successfully excised his own involvement with it. This separation of the parts of his identity is the source of the lofty disdain of his later work which has earned him the role of bogeyman to many writers and theorists of the effects of colonisation. Even in *Enigma*, the question of race is carefully excluded from his self-narrativisation of his initial arrival in England. Forgetting becomes a crucial part of Naipaul's narrative of arrival. It is not the deliberately foregrounded distortion of memory that we see in *Midnight's Children*. It is rather a record of how the postcolonial migrant, with a self-image almost wholly derived from the coloniser, seeks to remove all traces of that subject position from his recollections. He admits to the suppression of memory. Whereas history is a crucial aspect of Rushdie's texts and memory is for him the key to the reconstruction of the migrant's distorted history, history for Naipaul is too grand a narrative to be associated with the colonial subject. In An *Area of Darkness* he expresses his belief that Indians can 'have no sense of history, for how then would they be able to squat amid their ruins, and which Indian would be able to read the history of his country for the last thousand years without anger and pain?'[15] History becomes instead the safe and sanitised record of events and dates which assist him in his own conquest of Englishness: history decontextualised and depoliticised.

It is only through the persona of writer that Naipaul is able to achieve at least a partial coming to terms with his own history and identity. He can no longer conceive of this persona in terms of its western, colonial designation as the record of the development of inward sensibility. By coming to terms with this realisation, he opens the way for memories of his Port of Spain childhood to reassemble and override the attempt to construct a narrative around the fantasy of a sophisticated metropolitan existence. His subject now becomes not the writer's inner development and introspection but 'the world I contained within myself, the worlds I lived in' (*Enigma*, 135). Through the fog of obscurity that has blurred his sense of location comes an image of the street where he lived as a child.

The part that objects and possessions play in the art of memory is again imbued with that same sense of change and decay for Naipaul. Rushdie's own attitude to such keys to memory is that they do possess a value but that that value can diminish the further the object recedes from the place of 'belonging'. In *Shame* he writes that:

> all migrants leave their pasts behind, although some try to pack it into bundles and boxes – but on the journey something seeps out of the treasured mementoes... until even their owners fail to recognise them, because it is the fate of migrants to be stripped of history. (*S*, 63)

But the effects of such objects can be enormously important, as was the photograph of his Bombay childhood home to Rushdie's recollection of India in *Midnight's Children*. For Naipaul, 'photographs' and 'snapshots' are 'melancholy in their effect: each snapshot, capturing a moment of time, with all its unconsidered details, forcing one to think of the tract of time that had followed, and being a kind of memento mori' (*Enigma*, 173).

Naipaul is further able to distance himself from the past and some of its harsher lessons by using the figures of Pitton, the estate gardener, and Alan, the failed writer, as people through whose lives he can fictionalise his own experiences of alienation. The text itself is subtitled 'a novel in five sections' which suggests a desire for distance from his subject. He speaks of being distanced from the reality of his experience in the past, yet the text itself engages in a process of concealment that purports to be revelation. It is as if after the confessional section of 'The Journey', Naipaul feels obliged to examine alienation, solitude and social discomfort through others. It then perhaps becomes as true of Naipaul as he believes it is of Alan, that 'one could never touch the true person' (*Enigma*, 264).

Naipaul acknowledges towards the end of his narrative that men need history to help them understand who they are, but concludes rather feebly that it can remain in the heart, presumably unexplored and unexpressed, because 'it is enough that there is something there' (*Enigma*, 318). It is as if Naipaul has started to rake over painful and long-suppressed memories but cannot write the full narrative of that life because he has so fully entered into a wholly other identity. To attempt to write the whole story would perhaps occasion the dislocation of the schizophrenic Gibreel.

What then of Rushdie's decision to attempt such a task? How can a text hold such separations within it? As previously mentioned in the discussion of *Grimus*, *The Satanic Verses* illustrates Bakhtin's ideas on how dreams can disrupt text and characterisation; where man 'ceases to mean only one thing' and 'ceases to coincide with himself.' For Gayatri Spivak, the text's disrupted narratives and dream sequences are indicative of the disruptions caused to identity by imperialism. In 'Reading *The Satanic Verses*', she states that:

> the confident breaching of the boundaries between dream and waking in the text – not merely in the characters – ... can earn for *The Satanic Verses* a critic's subtitle: 'Imperialism and Schizophrenia'. Not because empire, like capital, is abstract, but because empire messes with identity.[16]

Rushdie stated in a 1988 interview that the theme of schizophrenia in *The Satanic Verses* had been prompted by a close friend's suicide[17] and indeed his previously unpublished short story 'The Harmony of the Spheres' in *East, West* deals with the suicide of a man who, like Gibreel, is pursued by demons and eaten up by paranoia (*EW*, 125–46). But the theme is given a twist in *The Satanic Verses* by its association with forms of alienation specific to the post-colonial subject.

Saladin's identity has been disrupted from the outset. His voice-overs and his role in The Aliens Show are just the externalised forms of his reinvention. Underlying them is his desire for cultural assimilation and his obsessive pursuit of Englishness which alienates him from his father and from Zeeny. England and the British Empire may have defined themselves but Indianness, like the post-colonial subject, is defined by others, usually in negative terms. Saladin becomes subject to this process after his demonic transformation – the dehumanisation of the alien or other taken to its extreme. In the detention centre with the other designated aliens he experiences a nightmarish encounter with the manticore – a bizarre amalgam of different creatures, demonstrating the dehumanisation of the migrant's identity by the coloniser. 'They have the power of description, and we succumb to the pictures they construct' (*SV*, 168). Gibreel in his schizophrenic state sees this; sees 'fictions masquerading as real human beings' on the streets of London (*SV*, 192).

In *The Wretched of the Earth*, Frantz Fanon defined in the terms of the clinical psychologist what he called 'a regular and important mental pathology which is the direct product of oppression'.[18] Ashis Nandy in *The Intimate Enemy* sees the roots of this pathology embedded deep within the minds of both ruler and ruled. For Nandy, colonialism results in a division of the mind into the 'self' and the 'not self', mirrored, as mentioned earlier, in both the characterisations and the structural divisions between dream and waking.[19] Gibreel's inability to distinguish between dream and reality leads to his treatment for paranoid schizophrenia, while Saladin's demonic persona is seen by his friend Jumpy Joshi as 'psychological breakdown, loss of sense of self' (*SV*, 253). Both Nandy as theoretician and Rushdie as writer see this division as a defence mechanism on the part of the post-colonial subject. For Nandy, the subject becomes 'other' or alien to himself in order to, as he puts it, 'disaffiliate the violence and the humiliation he suffers from the essential constituent of his self', making his world 'partly dream-like or unreal'.[20] *The Satanic Verses* virtually paraphrases this: 'A being going through life can become so other to himself as to be another, discrete, severed from history' (*SV*, 288), while Gibreel's mental confusion illustrates the defensive impulse of the schizophrenic; 'his splitting of his sense of himself into two entities, one of which… by characterizing it as other than himself, [he] preserved, nourished, and secretly made strong' (*SV*, 340).

There is a striking similarity between the characterisation of Gibreel's dreamlike existence and Naipaul's unconscious fears about his situation in *The Enigma of Arrival*. The journey section of the text shows him experiencing a recurring dream which, like Gibreel's, seems to arise from the sense of cultural and geographic dislocation. Naipaul writes:

> In this dream there occurred always, at a critical moment in the dream narrative, what I can only describe as an explosion in my head. It was how every dream ended, with this explosion that threw me flat on my back, in the presence of people, in a street, in a crowded room, or wherever, threw me into this degraded position in the midst of standing people, threw me into the posture of sleep in which I found myself when I awakened. (*Enigma*, 93)

This description, his 'degraded position in the midst of standing people', gives an insight into the sense of inferiority experienced by the colonial subject in relation to authority; its public nature the index of all the humiliations of his situation. *The Satanic Verses* shows Gibreel prostrate on a number of occasions, usually waking up at the feet of Allie Cone. She seems to offer a temporary hope of reintegration for Gibreel, but both he and Naipaul are, ultimately, alone with themselves.

How then does the migrant avoid this disintegration? The earlier quotation from *The Satanic Verses*, which spoke of the migrant as severed from history, provides the clue to Rushdie's answer. Naipaul's position is to seek a clarity of viewpoint in the present through a disavowal of the migrant's hybridised cultural and historical situation. In *Midnight's Children*, Saleem Sinai declares that the 'awareness of oneself as a homogeneous entity in time, a blend of past and present, is the glue of personality, holding together our then and our now' (*MC*, 351). Saladin's pursuit of Englishness is a repression of his own personal and cultural history. He cuts down the walnut tree planted by his father to celebrate his birth, attempting to excise those years from the narrative of his existence. Zeeny's role is to show up the chasms in his re-invention of himself; the gaps between past and present through which his real self is slipping.

The crucial role that Rushdie assigns to Zeeny in the text is undercut somewhat by his presentation of her, and by the continuing tendency to demonise the female. Timothy Brennan senses that Rushdie's characterisations of women in *The Satanic Verses* are 'strangely demeaning',[21] but seems unable to pin down the cause of his reservations. *The Satanic Verses* shows Rushdie caught once again between the threat and the promise that women simultaneously seem to embody for him. The body of Tavleen, the Sikh extremist who causes the explosion that destroys the hijacked aircraft, is in many ways the ultimate figuring of woman as destruction in Rushdie's fiction: 'they could all see the arsenal of her body, the grenades like extra breasts nestling in her cleavage, the gelignite taped around her thighs' (*SV*, 81). Beauty and destructiveness, fear and desire, appear simultaneously as they did with Bird-Dog, Liv Jones and Parvati.

Gibreel is presented as both the 'beneficiary' and the 'victim' of female emotional and sexual generosity (*SV*, 26) – a victim in the sense that he is allowed to continue philandering and break-ing hearts without being made aware of the consequences of his actions. But is this just a piece of sophistry on Rushdie's part? To locate Gibreel between the twin dilemmas apparently offered by unencumbered sexual gratification is to exonerate him from ulti-mate responsibility for his actions; conscience, like gratification, becomes the gift and the responsibility of woman.

In his account of the Satanic Verses 'affair', Malise Ruthven is keen to suggest correspondences between the characters of Pamela Lovelace and Rushdie's first wife, Clarissa and Allie Cone and the Australian travel writer Robyn Davidson with whom Rushdie was involved before his second marriage to Marianne Wiggins.[22] Such an overlaying of text onto life is rarely particularly useful, but in this instance it may shed some light on the depiction of Zeeny Vakil and her crucial role as the 'saviour' of Saladin's Indian self.

Zeeny is a doctor, a part-time art critic who mirrors Rushdie's own views on artistic eclecticism, and a committed and unselfish political activist to boot. The fact that Ruthven hazards no sug-gestion of a correspondence between Zeeny and a 'live' woman in Rushdie's own past or present contributes to the general air that Zeeny has of being a fantasy figure, strangely two-dimensional and not very far removed in her presentation from the 'lurid painting of a bare-breasted myth-woman' that hangs in the Shaandaar Café (*SV*, 184). The conflict apparent in Rushdie's presentation of women is given a different dimension in Zeeny. One does not have to doubt the sincerity of Rushdie's belief in the force of love as the 'prime mover' in effecting the rebirth of identity to feel that Zeeny's role is too comfortably appropriate. It diverts attention from the fact that the crucially important love affair for Saladin is the one between himself and his father, Changez. The scenes around the latter's deathbed convey a poignancy that is only hinted at in Zeeny's offer to Saladin at the end of the text. As the narrator declares, 'to fall in love with one's father after the long angry decades was a serene and beautiful feeling; a renewing, life-giving thing' (*SV*, 523).

The reconstruction of Saladin's identity cannot take place on his initial return to Bombay, because at that time his old self is effectively dead. His subsequent experiences in London and the death of his father provide the necessary impetus for the change, which has to be a rebirth rather than a reinvention. His father withholds the gift of his lamp; the lamp that had been imbued with magic for the young Saladin, until they are reconciled on Changez's deathbed. Parentless children and also the possibilities of 'multiple' parentages have always been a symbol of the post-colonial subject's division from parts of his or her own history in Rushdie's writing. Flapping Eagle in *Grimus* who is 'Born-from-Dead', Omar Khayyam Shakil and his three mothers in *Shame*, the confusion that surrounds Saleem's birth in *Midnight's Children* – all separate the individual protagonists from their pasts, the past which Saladin allows to regather around him in India.

The themes of the birth of new identities and of a new religion are interlinked in the text. Saladin argues for flexibility from the Sikh separatists who hijack the aeroplane – he asks this particular 'idea' to compromise, to reshape its imperatives. Islam, if one accepts the episode of the 'satanic verses', accepts and then rejects the notion of flexibility. Saladin himself is the embodiment of flexibility – moulding himself to the shape of 'Englishness'. His identity in the early stages of the text is mirrored in the form of the dream-city of 'Jahilia' (meaning literally 'ignorance'; the period before Islam). Jahilia is a city of sand, its 'newly invented permanence' (*SV*, 94) a metaphor for the attempts to construct a solid identity made by such as Saladin.

Here again, the text links to Naipaul's project in its concern with journeys and arrivals. For the previously nomadic people of Jahilia, 'the journeying itself was home' (SV, 94). Where Naipaul's text suggests that the certainty of having 'arrived' is illusory and even unattainable, *The Satanic Verses* asserts that 'for the migrant... the point is to arrive' (SV, 94). The concept of 'arrival' is multi-layered for the migrant. On one level both Naipaul and Rushdie speak of a ritual central to the formation of the artist's identity – a ritual encapsulated by Janet Frame in *The Envoy from Mirror City*:

> Standing with my luggage on the grimy London steps I felt
> fleetingly at the back of my mind the perennial drama of
> the Arrival and its place in myth and fiction, and I again
> experienced the thrilling sense of being myself excavated
> as reality, the ore of the polished fiction.[23]

On another, there is 'arrival' in the sense of social acceptance.
This is the feeling that eludes Naipaul as he ponders the significance of the de Chirico painting entitled 'The Enigma of Arrival'
and the mental image it conjures up for him of the migrant who
'lose[s] his sense of mission' and 'know[s] only that he was lost'
(*The Enigma of Arrival*, 92), while for Rushdie 'arrival' is the
literal end of the migrant's 'journey', be it a physical or psychological one.

To return to Bakhtin's ideas expressed in *Problems of Dostoevsky's Poetics* is to see a way of theorising the contrast in
Rushdie's and Naipaul's narratives of migrant experience. Bakhtin
saw what he termed the dialogic form as possible only in certain
examples of the novel form, rather than in poetry or drama. Its
achievement was to allow the free play of a multiplicity of voices
within the text which did not appear to be subordinated to the
controlling authority or voice of the writer. Such dialogic forms
could then clearly offer opportunities for more subversive and
politically liberating works. In opposition to the polyphony of
the dialogic form is the monologic; a univocal form where all
ideas and characterisations are manifestly subject to the writer's
own voice.

Naipaul's narrative is clearly monologic; no tensions are
registered in the surface smoothness of the language and all disruptions caused to his identity by the process of migration are
nevertheless controlled and filtered through this univocal text.
Language itself is not seen as the site of struggle when, as elsewhere, Naipaul is content to operate within the dominant discourse of 'Eng. Lit'. He believes that his migration from Trinidad
to England has 'given [him] the English language as [his] own'
(*Enigma*, 52).

It would be problematic to assert that Rushdie achieves a
contrastingly successful implementation of the dialogic form.

Even though *The Satanic Verses* is largely concerned with who is the controlling power and guiding force behind any utterance, the very foregrounding of the argument and Rushdie's own intrusive authorial interventions make it difficult to argue that he steps back from the narrative in any true sense. That aside, the idea of polyphony and a multiplicity of textual voices is at the heart of Rushdie's ideas about fiction and his own belief in its ultimate validity as a vehicle for social and political ideas. Indeed, Philip Engblom argues that 'In *The Satanic Verses* every one of the Menippean elements that Bakhtin so carefully enumerates is so prominently on display that it would not be far wrong to call the novel a modern Menippean satire.'[24]

The concept of multiple narrative voices is one Rushdie embraced when defending *The Satanic Verses* in his 1990 Herbert Read Lecture, 'Is Nothing Sacred?': 'Literature', he writes, 'is the one place in any society where, within the secrecy of our own heads, we can hear voices talking about everything in every possible way' (*IH*, 429). Beyond the wider arguments of those voices is the disruption and subversion of language itself; something of which the dialogic form is also capable. In *The Satanic Verses*, Jumpy Joshi, socialist and amateur poet, is infuriated with the lawyer Hanif Johnson whom he feels is unwilling to grasp the importance of this issue of language for the migrant:

> Hanif was in perfect control of the languages that mattered: sociological, socialistic, black- radical, anti-anti-anti-racist, demagogic, oratorical, sermonic: the vocabularies of power. [But you bastard you rummage in my drawers and laugh at my stupid poems. The real language problem: how to bend it shape it, how to let it be our freedom, how to repossess its poisoned wells, how to master the river of words of time of blood: about all that you haven't got a clue]. (*SV*, 281)

One of the important features of Rushdie's texts is that, even within the course of such a diatribe, he is playing with words, the structure of sentences, and attempting to reclaim some of the coloniser's preconceptions about migrants: in this instance the rivers ˙of blood that Enoch Powell prophesied would foam through the streets of Britain if the immigration laws were not changed.

Rushdie's controversial use of the name 'Mahound' for his dream-prophet is intended as a similar rebuff to the Powellian impulse in man – 'To turn insults into strengths, whigs, tories, Blacks all chose to wear with pride the names they were given in scorn' (SV, 93). The text's own movement through the reinvention of identity, to rebirth, is linked to Jumpy's desire to rework Powell's metaphor. To be that which is designated as 'other' is to be reinvented. To stem the tide of abuse and remake the abuser's language anew is to be privy to a rebirth.

Ultimately, it is the deployment of polyphony that provides the opportunity for effecting a positive reconstruction of the divided migrant identity. The use of a novelistic form which can contain a multiplicity of voices, allows for the establishment of an identity that is inclusive rather than exclusive; capable of embracing past and present, memory and history, rather than, as is the case with the univocal *Enigma*, having to renounce or dissociate oneself from one's origins. For Rushdie, the implications of this strategy extend beyond the discussion of migrant identity to define our expectations of literature itself. As he puts it in 'Is Nothing Sacred?', 'the only privilege literature deserves – and this privilege it requires in order to exist – is the privilege of being the arena of discourse, the place where the struggle of languages can be acted out (*IH*, 427). Rushdie is here echoing the sentiments of the writer Carlos Fuentes who, shortly after the 'affair' blew up, applauded the Bakhtinian dialogism of Rushdie's text:

> Rushdie's work perfectly fits the Bakhtinian contention that ours is an age of competitive languages. The novel is the privileged arena where languages in conflict can meet, bringing together, in tension and dialogue, not only opposing characters, but also different historical ages, social levels, civilisations and other, dawning realities of human life. In the novel, realities that are normally separated can meet, establishing a dialogic encounter, a meeting with the other.'[25]

In his defence of *The Satanic Verses* in his essay 'In Good Faith', Rushdie speaks of 'the process of hybridization which is the novel's most crucial dynamic' (*IH*, 403). In part it is a dynamic created from the dialogism of multiple textual voices – dissenting, lying, asserting identity against a 'tide' of demonisation; voices once rehearsed discordantly in *Grimus*, now harmonised into a work that reflects the Sufi ideal of diversity within unity and asserts its multiform nature as its defining characteristic.

Haroun and the Sea of Stories

THE title of the closing chapter of *The Satanic Verses*, 'A Wonderful Lamp', refers to the object that has come to symbolise the relationship of Saladin Chamcha to his father, Changez: the death-bed gift that ultimately represents for both of them the magic of love regained. Yet in the final confrontation of Saladin with the schizophrenic and madly jealous Gibreel Farishta, the lamp is used as the hiding place for a gun, with which Gibreel first threatens Saladin, and then commits suicide. The role of the lamp in these closing scenes of the text is crucial for reinforcing Saladin's sense that the lamp's former ability to summon up images from *The Thousand and One Nights*, where 'the true djinns of old had the power to open the gates of the Infinite, to make all things possible, to render all wonders capable of being attained' (*SV*, 546) has now been consigned to that distant place labelled 'childhood', while its owner contends with the simultaneous terrors and banalities of his adult existence.

Looking back at this scene from the standpoint of *Haroun and the Sea of Stories*, and with the knowledge of all the intervening traumas that have assailed its author, it is inviting to see Rushdie in the position of Saladin at the end of *The Satanic Verses*, standing as he does 'at the window of his childhood' (*SV*, 546) looking back at a dead father and a place that is no longer home, but unlike Saladin, choosing to step back through that divide for however brief a respite from adulthood. What was for Saladin 'no more than an old and sentimental echo' (*SV*, 547) of a bygone era seems nevertheless to draw his creator to it when faced with the terrible prospect of 'narrative closure' implicit in a sentence of death.

In a 1991 interview with the poet James Fenton, Rushdie spoke of writing *Haroun* partly in fulfilment of a promise to his son Zafar, 'that the next book I wrote would be one he might enjoy reading'.[1] He speaks movingly of the strength of this 'imperative',[2] but *Haroun* itself is more than merely a response to a young boy's demand to be entertained. It is the coalescing, in the guise of a narrative for children, of debates about freedom of expression and the liberty of the artistic imagination, the re-working of old stories into new and the status of popular culture. All this, within a framework that effectively allegorises a very personal crisis in the lives of a father and son.

If Rushdie did indeed look back longingly through the window of his own childhood in creating *Haroun*, then the text's recreation of that magical realm must also be seen to offer the writer the solace of childhood; its possibilites and seeming limit-lessness. The fascination that childhood exerts over Rushdie's imagination is reflected in his 1992 monograph on the film *The Wizard of Oz*.[3] His subtitle for this extended appreciation of the classic film, 'A Short Text About Magic', seems to refer not only to the marvels of 1930s Hollywood special effects, but also to the nature of the rosy glow that colours adult recreations of child-hood, from *The Wizard of Oz* through to *Haroun* itself. A recol-lection of Rushdie's dying father is the starting point of this monograph – a claim made by him in his last illness that he still possessed a copy of a story written by the ten year-old Rushdie entitled 'Over the Rainbow' (*WO*, 9). Without at first stating them overtly, Rushdie quickly sets up the obvious philosophical links between his own response to *The Wizard of Oz* and one of the many messages implicit in *Haroun*, namely that it is 'a film whose driving force is the inadequacy of adults, and how the weakness of grown-ups forces children to take control of their own destinies, and so, ironically, grow up themselves' (*WO*, 10). That a similar scenario was at the back of Rushdie's own mind when constructing *Haroun* is borne out by further statements made to James Fenton the previous year:

Children blame themselves for the misfortunes that befall the adults in their lives. It is a place to write from. A terrible

thing happens to a father, the child blames himself and
wishes to rescue the father. And in the novel not just the
father, but the whole world, while he's doing it, and why
not?[4]

Haroun Khalifa does indeed take charge of the dire situation
that confronts his father Rashid; the total loss of the 'Shah of
Blah's prodigious storytelling abilities. Through the medium of
fiction, Rushdie attempts a partial exorcism of the feelings of responsibility that he senses his own son might feel, if not for his
father's enforced exile, then perhaps for his parents' divorce. It is
also the act by which he overcomes the writing block imposed on
his own imagination by the dictates of the fatwa. As he tells
Fenton, 'I spent an awful lot of time thinking I would never write
again.'[5] Haroun's mother, who runs away with a neighbour at
the beginning of the story, is finally reunited with her husband
and son in what is, from the child's perspective at least, a piece of
blatant if understandable wish-fulfilment. Haroun is allotted the
role of prime mover in the narrative, ensuring that his parents
have grown up sufficiently to become reconciled to one another
and, in the case of Rashid, to re-engage with the sources of imagination that reside at the heart of childhood.

Haroun is not the first instance of Rushdie exploring the
drying-up of the sources of imagination in a storyteller. As far
back as *Midnight's Children* we witness the disintegration of
Saleem Sinai's father, Ahmed, whose power to entertain his son
with his storytelling diminishes as he becomes increasingly
bound up with the problems of reality:

> a more depressing indication of his withdrawal from family
> life was that he rarely told us bedtime stories any more,
> and when he did we didn't enjoy them, because they had
> become ill-imagined and unconvincing. Their subject-
> matter was still the same, princes goblins flying horses and
> adventures in magic lands, but in his perfunctory voice we
> could hear the creaks and groans of a rustling, decayed
> imagination. (*MC*, 201–2)

Rashid's own powers have deserted him through the twin traumas of his wife's departure and his son's subsequent irritation

with the realm of unreality that his father seems to inhabit – 'What's the use of stories that aren't even true?'[6] The text both sets out to answer the question in the course of the narrative, by recounting the fantastic adventures of Haroun, and effectively *is* the answer to the question in itself.

So what is the nature of Rushdie's defence of the literary imagination in *Haroun*? In terms of narrative technique, aspects of Haroun's home life, elements of his father's speech and products of the latter's imagination become incorporated into the fantastic experiences that unfold around the child. The multi-layered end-product is the fantastic made 'real' within the confines of a literary fantasy. 'No ifs, no buts'; the standard parental response to a child's questioning of authority becomes incorporated into the story in the forms of Iff, the Water Genie, and Butt, the Hoopoe. 'Ifs' and 'buts' have a place in the child's perception of reality. They not only contest adult opinion on the primacy of their own view of the world, but (and here we move into one of the adult 'gears' of the text) also assert the validity of questioning and dissent on a wider scale within society.

In addition the reader familiar with Rushdie's respect for Sufi mysticism can detect here a dovetailing of the child's way of experiencing reality with the Sufi method of apprehending 'truth'. Kenneth Cragg in *The Call of the Minaret* describes the path of the Sufi mystic towards truth in a way that mirrors Haroun's own journey towards accepting the 'reality' of the imagination:

> Mysticism believes in an alternative way to truth *beyond reason and revelation dogmatically defined.* It discounts what Muslim theology calls aql, 'intellect', and naql, 'transmitted truth' and concentrates on kashf, 'discovery', in which the meaning of faith and truth is given in experimental immediacy to the seeking soul.[7]

Haroun himself also becomes further linked to the Sufi symbolism that first surfaced in *Grimus*, by choosing the hoopoe to be his companion and guide. Just as the hoopoe leads the thirty birds towards their leader in 'Attar's *Conference of the Birds,* so Butt the Hoopoe leads Haroun to his journey's end.

The primary task facing Haroun in the text is the cleansing and release of the Oceans of the Streams of Story which, like the source of stories within Rashid, is in imminent danger of drying up due to the evil plans of Khattam-Shud. Khattam-Shud is a Hindi expression which Rushdie glosses with a translation as 'completely finished' or 'over and done with', here representative of this malign figure's desire to impose silence upon free expression, imaginative or otherwise.

Glossaries aside, one cannot help but make a connection between Khattam-Shud and Rushdie's own chief persecutor, Khomeini; the voice of the fatwa that seeks to impose the most final of silences on Rushdie. The likenesses between Khattam-Shud and Khomeini, and between the Chupwala army and a common image of a fundamentalist Islamic society such as Iran, become more pronounced as the story progresses. The army resides in the Twilight Strip, wrapped in 'black tents' (*H*, 101) which call to mind the burqas that seem to western eyes to imprison Islamic women. The Chupwalas also worship the idol Bezaban, a 'colossus carved out of black ice' (*H*, 101), surely representative of the Black Stone, the sacred Ka'bah, the holiest place at the centre of Islam's holiest city, Mecca. It is important to remember that the publication of *Haroun* predated Rushdie's temporary 'conversion' to Islam and was fuelled in large part by understandable animosities towards the threats of his persecutors. The irony of these images at the heart of a 'children's' narrative is that in some respects they surpass in their allegorical literalness the obscurer offences against Islam in *The Satanic Verses*.

Such descriptions amply illustrate the dual child/adult nature of the text. Even when the narrative seems not to be prodding its older readers into an awareness of its allegories, there is still a tension between aspects of the narrative and its intended audience. Is 'encoded', here used more than once, a word that naturally forms part of a child's vocabulary? An adult critic perhaps inevitably reads *Haroun* in the light of its author's plight, with an eye on possible correspondences between real and fictional entities, such as fill the pages of *Shame*. But perhaps part of this curious duality actually serves to highlight the 'child's' reading of the text as representative of a critical innocence that the adult can no longer share.

'Snooty' Buttoo, who hires Rashid to entertain prospective supporters in an election campaign, takes the protagonists to his houseboat, aptly named 'Arabian Nights Plus One'. There he shows Rashid a copy of 'the entire collection of tales known as *The Ocean of the Streams of Story*' (*H*, 51). Rushdie makes no mention in *Haroun*, even in his glossary of names, that this alludes to an actual literary artefact. Where he does do so is in *The Satanic Verses*, where it serves again as a source of artistic enterprise, though of a rather different nature. Film producer S. S. 'Whisky' Sisodia has made his name and fortune from 'a string of box office hits based on old fables drawn from the *Katha-Sarit-Sagar* compendium – the 'Ocean of the Streams of Story', longer than the Arabian Nights and equally as fantasticated' (*SV*, 342). The endless possibilities for recuperating old stories into new, in this instance an epic of ancient Sanskrit literature, the work of the poet Somadeva from *c.* AD 1000, is figured in *The Satanic Verses*, not only in Sisodia's use of the *Katha-Sarit-Sagar* but also in Gibreel's success in the 'theologicals' where stories from Hindu mythology are endlessly recuperated through the Bombay film industry. The ocean of the ancient epic becomes visualised by Rushdie into a literal sea of fiction:

> Different parts of the Ocean contained different sorts of stories, and as all the stories that had ever been told and many that were still in the process of being invented could be found here, the Ocean of the Streams of Story was in fact the biggest library in the universe. (H, 72)

The very fluidity of Rushdie's image, playing in part on the use of sea journeys as a narrative connecting device in the original stories,[8] reinforces the interconnectedness of old and new stories apparent in all of Rushdie's writing, with the two literally flowing in and out of one another.

So has Rushdie finally, with *Haroun*, embraced wholeheartedly the label of postmodernist writer? Is the concept of the ocean of the streams of story a visualisation of Barthes's authorless, postmodern text, 'a multidimensional space in which a variety of writings, none of them original, blend and clash... a tissue of quotations drawn from the innumerable centres of culture'?[9] Rushdie's image of the Ocean quoted above is careful to stress the continuing potential for originality in literary art, while elsewhere he urges us to redefine our notion of 'originality' as something between the poles of 'pure' innovation and postmodern pastiche. 'Nothing comes from nothing', he has said. 'This is, to my surprise, called "postmodernism". It is impossible to believe that anything in history comes from no roots.'[10] While this may be something of a reductive view of postmodernism on Rushdie's part, it does highlight his belief that the inevitably hybridised end-product of the clash of ancient and modern should not in itself be condemned as proof of postmodern 'unoriginality'. Iff the Water Genie reinforces this idea when he tells *Haroun* that 'no story comes from nowhere; new stories are born from old – it is the new combinations that make them new' (*H*, 86). Both the art itself and the artist's identity reflect one another in their composite construction.

Though the text of *Haroun* displays Rushdie's engagement and fascination with elements of popular culture, it also demonstrates that for the author this is not merely a matter of applauding all that is current without regard to questions of 'value'. Significantly, the Ocean requires purification as well as 'unplugging'. Two particular pollutants singled out in the text are 'popular romances' that 'have become just long lists of shopping expeditions. Children's stories also. For instance, there is an outbreak of talking helicopter anecdotes' (*H*, 83), a clear reference to the Duchess of York's creation of Budgie the talking helicopter!

At the other end of the scale from 'shopping and fucking' novels and the literary exploits of the British royal family is the neglected 'Old Zone' (*H*, 86), that we are encouraged to think of as the region of traditional storytelling of the likes of *The Thousand and One Nights*. The text also displays its indebtedness to western realist novels, particularly apparent in the depiction of P2C2E House which recalls Dickens's Circumlocution Office in *Little Dorrit*, an image Rushdie has admitted to admiring.[11] It is:

a huge building from which whirrs and clanks were constantly heard, and inside which were concealed one thousand
and one Machines Too Complicated To Describe which controlled the Processes Too Complicated To Explain. (*H*, 88)

The effect of these diverse projects and influences on the
narrative itself is the creation of a text that takes many of the
features of Rushdie's earlier work – the fascination with film
techniques, the rhymes and jingles, the mimicry – to their extreme until it becomes what could be called 'textual animation'.
James Fenton remarked of *Haroun* that 'not all the intended
mimicry comes across on the page. One would expect the book,
in normal circumstances, to lead on to a film'.[12] Indeed, this is the
closest Rushdie has yet come to creating a work of literature so
visually imagined that it lends itself totally to filmic representation.

There is a particularly cartoon-like quality to many of its
scenes, where the words on the page scramble to convey the
speed and particularity that a thousand sequenced animations
flitting across a screen can provide. At the Bus Depot in the town
of G:

One driver would start his engine, adjust his mirrors, and
behave as if he were about to leave. At once a bunch of
passengers would gather up their suitcases and bedrolls
and parrots and transistor radios and rush towards him.
Then he'd switch off his engine with an innocent smile;
while on the far side of the courtyard, a different bus would
start up, and the passengers would start running all over
again. (*H*, 32)

A similar cartoon image can be found in *Shame* where Sufiya
Zinobia bursts free from her walled confines, leaving a body-
shaped hole in the bricks – a stock image from the 'Tom and
Jerry' cartoons.

The characters of Goopy and Bagha in *Haroun* are acknowledged by Rushdie as lifts from a 1915 short story by the Bengali
writer Upendrakishore Ray Chaudhuri[13] later immortalised by
his grandson, the eminent film director Satyajit Ray in his film
Goopy Gyne Bagha Byne (1969). Rushdie has commented that

in Bengal, Ray's film is as popular as *The Wizard of Oz* in the West (*IH*, 111), while the latter film is offered as an important source for the tone and style of *Haroun*:

> of all the movies, the one that helped me most as I tried to find the right voice for *Haroun* was *The Wizard of Oz*. The film's traces are there in the text, plain to see; in Haroun's companions there are clear echoes of the friends who danced with Dorothy down the Yellow Brick Road. (*WO*, 18)

I. M. D.Walrus (an obvious pun on the Beatles song and perhaps also a warning note against over-interpretation) is Rushdie's answer to the Wizard. He is the 'Grand Comptroller' (*H*, 58) who is at once at the heart of things, the fount of wisdom towards which the travellers journey, and the rather disappointing reality that awaits them at the end. Dorothy's ruby slippers that return her to the grey reality of Kansas are matched by the Walrus' gift of a bottled wish to Haroun, which he does indeed use to put the worlds of home and of Gup City to rights. The denouement allows Rushdie to empower the son to overcome the failings and weaknesses of the parents, and to provide at least a fictional happy ending to their situation.

The son is also the key to the father's reawakened storytelling abilities as Rushdie's promise to his son was for himself. At the close, the endless repetition and recuperation of stories is figured not just in abstract imagery of conceptual oceans, oceans of notions, but in Rashid's use of Haroun's adventures to entertain his audience. 'Haroun and the Sea of Stories' thus becomes a story within a story, standing at the centre of the 'hall of mirrors' that is the text itself.

Critical overview

FEW book-length studies of Rushdie's work have as yet been published, with scholarship in this area largely confined to essays in journals, periodicals and edited collections. M. D. Fletcher's collection of eighteen previously published articles and four specially commissioned pieces, *Reading Rushdie: Perspectives on the Fiction of Salman Rushdie* (1994), is an invaluable source of otherwise scattered essays, here grouped under the headings of each of Rushdie's major novels. Fletcher himself had previously published an annotated bibliography of essays on *Midnight's Children* and *Shame* in the *Journal of Indian Writing in English* (1991)[1] and *Reading Rushdie* extends this to a comprehensive thirty-five page bibliography of criticism in English on all the major texts, offering useful précis of the argument of each essay as a guide for the Rushdie scholar. The items listed in the bibliography date from 1981, when Rushdie's work first began to receive serious critical attention following the publication of *Midnight's Children,* to 1994.

The essays which appear in full in *Reading Rushdie,* the many more which are alluded to in the bibliography, as well as studies which have appeared subsequent to its publication can also be explored with regard to their primary thematic as well as textual focus. Examples of critical essays (beyond those discussed in detail in this study) which explore the western intertexts of Rushdie's writing, include Colin Smith's 'The Unbearable Lightness of Salman Rushdie',[2] M. Keith Booker's '*Finnegan's Wake* and *The Satanic Verses*: Two Modern Myths of the Fall',[3] and Patricia Merivale's 'Saleem Fathered by Oscar: Intertextual

Strategies in *Midnight's Children* and *The Tin Drum*',[4] while discussions of the eastern influences on both the language and structure of Rushdie's fiction include Wimal Dissanayake's 'Towards a Decolonized English: South Asian Creativity in Fiction'[5] and Ron Shepherd's '*Midnight's Children*: The Parody of an Indian Novel'.[6]

The treatment of history and its relation to issues of post-colonialism and postmodernism in Rushdie's fiction is explored in studies such as Sara Suleri's *The Rhetoric of English India*,[7] Uma Parameswaran's numerous essays on Rushdie's fiction collected under the title *The Perforated Sheet: Essays in Salman Rushdie's Art*,[8] David W. Price's 'Salman Rushdie's "Use and Abuse of History" in *Midnight's Children*',[9] David Birch's 'Postmodernist Chutneys'[10] and Srinivas Aravamudan's 'Being God's Postman is No Fun, Yaar'.[11]

The first major study of Rushdie's fiction to appear was Timothy Brennan's *Salman Rushdie and the Third World: Myths of the Nation* (1989).[12] As his title implies, Brennan is concerned with the relationship of Rushdie's fiction to discourses of nation-forming. While conceding that 'Third World' is an unhelpful and innacurate sociological category, he nevertheless employs the label of 'Third World cosmopolitan' to indicate Rushdie's complex allegiances and socio-cultural situation as a product of the Third World who is perceived as speaking primarily to the First.

Brennan sees Rushdie's self-characterisation of 'translated man' as crucial to a new strain of identity politics which asserts the positive value of migrancy and 'homelessness'. For Brennan, the new strand of fiction Rushdie has introduced to the canon of English Literature is removed from the decolonising, nationalist purposes of the first wave of anti-colonial writers such as Frantz Fanon and Amìlcar Cabral. Instead, Rushdie exhibits his own brand of metafiction and 'Third World postmodernism'[13] which is distinct from that of its primarily First World exponents. This style for Brennan is 'not so much an exception to as a different type of postmodern writing'[14] – exhibiting a playful, parodic exterior, but nevertheless centrally rooted in historical and political realities.

James Harrison's *Salman Rushdie* (1992), as well as offering its readers a potted account of Indian history, religion and politics, provides readings of the novels in relation to the established generic intertexts of European film, science fiction/fantasy, magical realism and modernism. As a textual study it traces the organising tropes and narrative strategies of Rushdie's fiction and argues that his writing espouses 'the need... for maximum flexibility, variety, variability, and intermingling or "hybridity" of human ideas and beliefs and customs.'[15]

In addition to such textual criticism there is now, of course, also a whole tranche of commentaries on the implications and repercussions of the fatwa. Brennan's and Harrison's studies, which postdate the fatwa, both touch on the subject of the 'Rushdie affair', but a number of texts deal with it as a separate issue and only venture into textual criticism in so far as it appears necessary for assessing the wider charge of blasphemy levelled at the author. These include Malise Ruthven's *A Satanic Affair*,[16] L. Appignanesi and S. Maitland eds, *The Rushdie File*,[17] W. J. Weatherby's *Salman Rushdie: Sentenced to Death*[18] and Dan Cohn-Sherbok ed., *The Salman Rushdie Controversy in Inter-Religious Perspective*.[19]

While critics feel the 'affair' is an unignorable aspect of Rushdie's existence, and is indeed itself becoming an intertext of his work as *Haroun* seems to suggest, the need to reassert the validity of his fictions *as* fictions and as the products of an innovative artist of international importance is self-evident. The remainder of this study will therefore concern itself with a closer examination of the critical claims made for the relationship of Rushdie's fiction to magical realism and postmodernism and the often problematic issue of gender politics as it arises in the texts, before reaffirming the claims made throughout for the positively hybridised nature of his work.

In the 1985 *Oxford Companion to English Literature*, edited by his friend Margaret Drabble, the Rushdie entry has the cross-reference 'see magical realism' beside his name.[20] This automatic identification of author and genre may seem unproblematic and, in many ways, magical realism would appear to be an obvious style for post-colonial writing to adopt, with Homi Bhabha referring to it as 'the literary language of the emergent post-colonial world'.[21] Jean-Pierre Durix in his essay 'Magic Realism in *Midnight's Children*' defines magical realist texts as being:

> closely linked with the social and political reality of the writer's homeland or region but ... also associat[ing] elements which are more often found in fairy tales or fantasy; without any warning, the narration suddenly leaves the conventions of verisimilitude to enter a world where everyday limitations can be infringed at will.[22]

Colonialism itself disrupts the historical 'narrative' of a country. Magical realism, with its juxtaposition of alternative realities and alternative versions of history, is a way of figuring this disruption.

In the case of *Midnight's Children*, colonialism occasions a double disruption in the text, through the presence and then the departure of the British. And if, as *The Satanic Verses* argues, colonialism induces a form of cultural schizophrenia in the post-colonial subject, then magical realism would seem to offer itself up as the literary expression of the disintegration and disruption that it causes to history and national identity. Just as *The Satanic Verses* speaks of the post-colonial psyche splitting, yet preserving and nourishing its separate divisions, so magical realism can show the cultural and national identity of post-colonial societies dividing and preserving their different versions of history. The conceptualisation of alternative realities allows for the exercise of a liberty within the text which can be politically liberating.

But it is possible to acknowledge the debt that Rushdie's writing owes to the forms of magical realism, without trusting the generic label to explain and contain the processes and achievements of his work. Aijaz Ahmad in his study *In Theory* is dismissive of the claims Bhabha makes for magical realism, seeing his statement as 'doubtful' and the pronouncement itself as characteristic of what he calls 'the metropolitan theory's inflationary rhetoric'.[23] In the wake of *The Satanic Verses* 'affair', Rushdie became keen to distance himself somewhat from this Latin American sector of influence. Before the storm broke he still appeared confused as to his relationship to magical realist writing, declaring that he saw his work as allied to surrealism rather than magical realism. It is one of many instances where Rushdie – perhaps because of his very hybridity – is unable to decide which strand of his make-up, Third or First World, he wishes to be allied to. He says:

> Of all the European artistic movements, surrealism is the one I most respond to, the idea that you have to make the world fresh, scratching away at the surface of expectation and habit… realism to me just means arriving at a defini-tion of the world which feels true. And in order to do that you might be required to use the most fantastical images… as long as the purpose is not to escape from the world but to capture it, that seems to me to be realism.[24]

This reiterates a point he makes at the end of *The Jaguar Smile* when he refutes the binary opposition of realism and fantasy:

> Unhappy endings might seem more realistic than happy ones, but reality often contained a streak of fantasy that realism… lacked. In the real world there were monsters and giants.(*JS*, 169)

He addresses the question again, indirectly, in a review of Gabriel García Márquez's *Chronicle of a Death Foretold*:

> *El realismo magical*, magical realism, at least as practised by Márquez, is a development out of Surrealism that ex-presses a genuinely 'Third World' consciousness. (*IH*, 301)

The complexity of Rushdie's stance derives from his belief at this stage that magical realism as much as traditional realism was capable of capturing the world in all its extremes and peculiari-ties. The definition and defence of magical realism proposed here are useful for judging the true nature of Rushdie's claims for the cultural and political validity of his own writing.

Rushdie has questioned assessments of *Midnight's Children* as a fantasy novel, comparing it to the responses of Indian read-ers who have seen it as 'a novel of history and politics. And memory'.[25]

'Third World' writers such as himself and Márquez take

what they require from the dominant discourses of powerful, colonial cultures and reshape it to serve their own ends. There is also the desire to be seen as more than a literary dilettante, playing with the form of the novel for no other reason than that he can and thus serving a discourse which ultimately addresses itself. He appears to be straining at the ties that bind him to postmodernity on the one hand and post-coloniality on the other.

Writing of the putative category of 'Commonwealth Literature', Rushdie makes a statement which has implications for the assessment and subsequent 'categorisation' of his own fiction:

> the creation of a false category can and does lead to excessively narrow, and sometimes misleading readings of some of the artists it is held to include; and again, the existence…
> of the beast distracts attention from what is actually worth looking at, what is actually going on.(*IH*, 63–4)

'Postmodernist' and 'magical realist' are not in themselves 'false' categories, if the plethora of theories that surround them is anything to go by. But they can, like 'Commonwealth Literature', serve as classifications that carry with them preordained ideas for readers – ideas that sometimes reinforce the sense of a lack of originality in contemporary literature. To label Rushdie's writing as postmodernist, magical realist or fantasist is often to deny its arguments, its formal innovativeness and its political dimension. What defies labelling or eschews the existing categories available must be reckoned with differently.

In attempting such a reassessment, it is first necessary to examine some of the confusions which Rushdie's work clearly presents to any critic intent on labelling it. The level of engagement of Rushdie's writing with the tropes of postmodernism is inevitably a major distraction for western critics. The occasions when Rushdie has himself entered into the debate about the relation of the writer's art to theory illustrate the confusion and ambivalence that surrounds this question. Cora Kaplan, in her essay 'The Feminist Politics of Literary Theory', recalls a discussion of the relationship between creative writing and theory at an ICA conference which Rushdie attended. Kaplan notes that Rushdie 'tended to see [theory's] uses in imaginative writing as marginal, pointing out that he took his models and examples from the popular storytellers still practising in the sub-continent'.[26] The discussion of *Midnight's Children* has already demonstrated how far Rushdie's work can be said to emerge from an oral tradition, but this disavowal of theoretical engagement seems somewhat disingenuous when one is confronted with the theoretical, let alone fictional intertextuality of such novels as *Midnight's Children* and *The Satanic Verses*.

Theories of postmodernism simultaneously offer a promise of validation for the post-colonial writer and a threat to his or her 'authority'. The 'postmodern condition' by Jean-François Lyotard's definition – simplifying to extremes as he puts it – is characterised by what he terms our 'incredulity towards metanarratives'.[27] We no longer subscribe to a totalising world view, so the arguments go, any view that formerly served to explain the world and man's relation to it. Centres of power are allegedly dispersed. In terms of art, acknowledgement of this breakdown of centred authority is mirrored in the now familiar techniques of postmodern literature – the 'death' of the author and concomitant valorisation of the role of the reader outlined by Roland Barthes, along with the concept of the intertextuality of all writing. Self-referentiality, unreliable narration, multiple voices, perspectives and endings are some of the forms in which this incredulity towards metanarratives finds expression in literature.

As mentioned earlier, *Midnight's Children* toys with the idea of using Padma to occupy the role of reader as designated by Barthes, while *Haroun* also appears to incorporate Barthes's ideas. Linda Hutcheon in *A Poetics of Postmodernism*, regards *Midnight's Children* as a prime example of what she terms 'historiographic metafiction', a term used to identify 'those well-known and popular novels which are both intensely self-reflexive and yet paradoxically also lay claim to historical events and personages.'[28] *The Satanic Verses* similarly displays Rushdie's awareness of the tropes of postmodernist discourse in its presentation of the apparent superficiality of contemporary existence. The schizophrenia at the heart of Gibreel's disintegration extends beyond Rushdie's arguments about migrant identity in the text to define an aspect of the postmodern world in which it is produced.

Fredric Jameson, in his essay 'Postmodernism and Consumer Society', isolates pastiche and schizophrenia as the two significant features of postmodernism. He singles out pastiche rather than parody, as the latter requires 'that still latent feeling that there exists something normal compared to which what is being imitated is rather comic'.[29] Rushdie has Saladin's co-mimic, Mimi Mamoulian, echo this sentiment in *The Satanic Verses*: 'I have read *Finnegan's Wake* and am conversant with postmodernist critiques of the West, e.g. that we have here a society capable only of pastiche: a "flattened world"' (*SV*, 261). Another theorist of postmodernity, Jean Baudrillard, also reinforces Jameson's pronouncements on the postmodern era when he declares in 'The Ecstasy of Communication' that 'we are now in a new form of schizophrenia.'[30] Like Gibreel himself, Baudrillard's schizo 'can no longer produce the limits of his own being, can no longer play nor stage himself'.[31]

As for *The Satanic Verses*' engagement with magical realism, the protagonists' crash-landing on the English coastline enables Rushdie to indulge in the kind of stylistic 'improvisation' that was one of the besetting sins of *Grimus*. Here, Gibreel is introduced to the aged Rosa Diamond, a figure straight out of Gabriel García Márquez with her history of passion, deceit and violence in Latin America. Interestingly, this is in many ways the least successful episode in the text, included more for its obvious literary resonances than for its links with the text's central themes. This suggests that Rushdie is genuflecting towards those non-Indian literary figures whose work he so admired, without necessarily wishing his own text to be regarded as part of that genre.

A similar strategy which speaks more of homage than discipleship is Rushdie's deployment of the trope of the labyrinth in *The Satanic Verses*. In his short story, 'The Garden of Forking Paths', Jorge Luis Borges provides a classic comparison of the art of the novelist and the Daedalean task of constructing a narrative:

Ts'ui Pên must have said once: *I am withdrawing to write a book*. And another time: *I am withdrawing to construct a labyrinth*. Everyone imagined two works; to no one did it occur that the book and the maze were one and the same thing.[32]

Rushdie's use of labyrinth, aside from offering echoes of Borges's magical realism, creates a similar effect to that produced by the storytelling technique employed in *Midnight's Children*; namely to convey an impression of loss of control within what is a tightly ordered narrative. Wendy Faris in *Labyrinths of Language* examines the use of the labyrinth in modern fiction both as structure and meaning, or effectively non-meaning; the paradigmatic inconclusiveness of the postmodern text. The urban landscape of London in the *The Satanic Verses* is presented as a centreless labyrinth which the hapless Gibreel attempts to navigate with his *A–Z*. Similar labyrinthine structures are allocated to the dream city of Jahilia and 'The Curtain' brothel, confusing those who venture into their complexities:

More than once [Gibreel] emerged, suffocating, from that subterranean world in which the laws of space and time had ceased to operate, and tried to hail a taxi; not one was willing to stop, however, so he was obliged to plunge back into that hellish maze, that labyrinth without a solution, and continue his epic flight. (*SV*, 201)

It is a 'text book' use of labyrinth as discussed by Faris – decentred, multicursal, offering options to the traveller (both Gibreel and Saladin are confronted with forking paths at critical moments in the text and choose, symbolically, the left-hand fork) and 'defying the laws of space and time'. Faris tells us that 'part of the labyrinth's attraction as an image results from its potential to oscillate between existence in space and time', seeming even 'to represent the very "shape of time"' itself.[33]

In both *Midnight's Children* and *The Satanic Verses*, the communication networks of advertising and cinema compete with the written word for man's attention and allegiance. The cinema screen becomes a symbol for the changing perspectives on 'reality' that are offered by the postmodern novel. In 'The Ecstasy of Communication', Baudrillard writes that 'today the scene and mirror no longer exist, there is a non-reflecting surface, an immanent surface where operations unfold – the smooth operational surface of communication'.[34] Like the cinema screen in *Midnight's Children* which disintegrates into a series of dots when the viewer gets too close to it, the riot of self-reflexiveness within the postmodern novel offers its readers the individualised elements of a once composite and unified whole.

Television, for Baudrillard, is 'the ultimate and perfect object for this new era'[35] and Rushdie again appears to keep in step with postmodernity by making a transition from the power of the Bombay talkies in *Midnight's Children* and *The Satanic Verses* to the transparency and levelling tendencies of a television-based culture:

> [Saladin] watched a good deal of television with half an eye, channel-hopping compulsively, for he was a member of the remote-control culture of the present... what a leveller this remote-control gizmo was... it chopped down the heavyweight and stretched out the slight until all the set's emissions, commercials, murders, game-shows, the thousand and one varying joys and terrors of the real and the imagined, acquired an equal weight. (*SV*, 405)

But, as with his relationship to magical realism, to acknowledge even this high degree of engagement in Rushdie's writing with the vocabulary of postmodernism is not to see the label of 'postmodern text' as sufficient in itself for explaining the various impulses and projects within his work. *The Satanic Verses* appears to revel in the truisms of postmodernity – the society of the spectacle, Mimi's flattened world, the centreless labyrinth through which the individual conducts his goalless quest. Indeed, M. D. Fletcher, after weighing up the pros and cons of the postcolonial versus the postmodern in Rushdie's work, plumps for a definition of the fiction as 'primarily postmodern'.[36]

But just as Brennan sees Third World cosmopolitanism as generally more positive and 'engaged' than First World postmodernism, *The Satanic Verses* itself is at odds with the often depressing and alienating conclusions of postmodern discourse. Rushdie's very facility with these debates becomes a way of refuting the ascendancy of their arguments as a means of explaining the world, and of demonstrating the seeds of a discontent with the self-congratulatory cleverness and even slick amorality of much postmodern discourse – both fictional and theoretical. Even in the midst of Mimi Mamoulian's apparent embrace of postmodernism, we can read Rushdie's own response to the discourse: 'When I become the voice of a bottle of bubble bath, I am entering flatland knowingly, understanding what I'm doing and why' (SV, 261). In an interview with David Brooks, Rushdie states that he is not interested in the idea of books as self-referential, closed systems[37] and that, for example, the oral narrative technique deployed in *Midnight's Children* is ' a form which is thousands of years old, and yet… has all the methods of the post-modernist novel… you become a post-modernist writer by being a very traditional one'.[38]

The denouement of *The Satanic Verses* provides a sense of closure and resolution that is uncharacteristic of postmodern novels in general and of Rushdie's earlier works in particular with their variously pessimistic and apocalyptic endings:

> Deprived of its connection with all relative Dimensions, the world of Calf Mountain was slowly unmaking itself, its molecules and atoms breaking, dissolving, quietly vanishing into primal, unmade energy. (G, 253)

> cracking now, fission of Saleem, I am the bomb in Bombay, watch me explode, bones splitting breaking beneath the awful pressure of the crowd, bag of bones falling down down down. (MC, 463)

> And then the explosion comes, a shockwave that demolishes the house, and after it the fireball of her burning, rolling outwards to the horizon like the sea, and last of all the cloud, which rises and spreads and hangs over the nothingness of the scene. (S, 286)

It seemed that in spite of all his wrongdoing, weakness, guilt – in spite of his humanity – he was getting another chance. There was no accounting for one's good fortune, that was plain. There it simply was, taking his elbow in its hand. 'My place', Zeeny offered. 'Let's get the hell out of here.' (SV, 547)

The Satanic Verses also demonstrates an increasing insistence on the importance and value of human relationships, resisting the alienating and selfish individualism of late eighties Britain under Mrs Torture. Zeeny's hand on Saladin's arm offers not only the hope of a relationship that is emotionally fulfilling, but one that, through her nationality and her cultural and political interests is intended to help validate Saladin's past and reassemble his fragmented identity.

The previous chapter raised the issue of Zeeny's impossible correctness while, as the discussions of G*rimus* and *Shame* have indicated, Rushdie's self-appointed status as champion of women in the face of religious, political and cultural constraints on their liberty cannot stand unchallenged. It is perhaps further evidence of the collision of east and west in his identity that western liberal feminist politics and eastern anxieties over female sexual authority and freedom seem to exist side-by-side in his work.[39]

Shame, in particular, has attracted critical commentary for its 'sexually overdetermined'[40] depictions and 'patriarchal fear'[41] of women. *Haroun* is equally interesting as the text which follows *The Satanic Verses* and similarly valorises the importance of familial and other relations. So at odds with Rushdie's own situation at the time of writing, *Haroun* nevertheless insists on an ending that offers a comparable degree of closure to *The Satanic Verses* and the resumption of family roles. (Here, the faithless female has the eventual good grace to return to her abandoned husband and son.)

Such a contrived 'happy ending' may seem to do nothing more than bow to a narrative convention in children's fiction. But in its 'adult' form in *The Satanic Verses* it marks an important and distinct move towards a literature that affirms the culture and identity of the post-colonial subject. It is in assessing

The Satanic Verses from amidst the wreckage of home and professional life in his essay 'In Good Faith' that Rushdie embraces the concept of hybridity wholeheartedly:

> *The Satanic Verses* celebrates hybridity, impurity, intermingling, the transformation that comes of new and unexpected combinations of human beings, cultures, ideas, politics, movies, songs. It rejoices in mongrelization and fears the absolutism of the Pure. (*IH*, 394)

As previously indicated in the Contexts and Intertexts section, recent post-colonial theory has attempted to engage with the concept of hybridity as it affects and informs post-colonial literature. The Indo-Anglian novel is regarded by Anuradha Dingwaney Needham as a 'peculiarly hybrid cultural/textual form'[42] while by 1990, Homi Bhabha was declaring in 'DissemiNation' that *The Satanic Verses* heralded 'the emergence of a hybrid national narrative'.[43] Such hybrid writing offers a challenge to existing standards of critical assessment and defies existing modes of categorisation. Bhabha had himself made it clear in 'Representation and the Colonial Text' that neither Leavisian discourse with its normative tendencies, nationalist criticism with its leanings towards essentialism, nor ideological analysis on the Althusserian model was equipped to critique and theorise post-colonial writing – chiefly because each of these methodologies has its own agenda, whether acknowledged or not.[44]

The acceptance of hybridity as a defining characteristic of both the post-colonial artist and his/her art allows for the circumvention of this critical triptych. The authors of *The Empire Writes Back* certainly see it this way. They see both the displeasure of nationalist critics at the lack of true authentic 'Indianness' in Rushdie's work, and the blindness of the European critics who are oblivious to its presence, as indicative of the failure to recognise hybridity as a positive cultural form rather than an expression of artistic fragmentation or confusion.[45] Hybridity, for Ashcroft, Griffiths and Tiffin, is 'the primary characteristic of all post-colonial texts',[46] though by the time they come to compile *The Post-Colonial Studies Reader* they are arguing that 'hybridity has been sometimes misinterpreted... as an alternative and absolute category to which all post-colonial forms inevitably subscribe'.[47] The latter revised position is perhaps an indication of the extent to which the concept of hybridity has become something of a dominant orthodoxy in contemporary post-colonial theory, an orthodoxy which Ashcroft *et al.* may be reluctant to valorise unduly.

Without instituting hybridity as an all-encompassing label for all forms of post-colonial writing, it is still arguably a useful term for defining as well as describing Rushdie's work. As such, each of the facets of a text such as *Midnight's Children* which have been variously attributed to the dominant cultural form of postmodernism – its self-reflexiveness, its allusive style, its use of traditional models – is not in itself *the* defining characteristic of his work, but rather representative of the whole as a unified, hybrid entity. The end product goes beyond the pastiche and inversion of postmodernity's flattened world in its unique demonstration of the discrete and even conflicting cultural influences that bear on Rushdie's writing, and which have been explored in the preceding chapters. As Ashcroft *et al.* put it, 'The interleaving of practices will produce new forms even as older forms continue to exist.'[48] The hybrid text is an artistic production which, like the artist himself who is both a product of colonialism and an exemplar of post-coloniality, displays simultaneously its indebtedness to other cultural forms, and its originality.

As 'In Good Faith' asserts, *The Satanic Verses* plays a crucial role in the assertion of hybridity as a positive and distinct characteristic. As previously mentioned, it toys with postmodernism's definitions of the world and the text, but the text itself strains against these strictures and pronouncements, creating the 'crucial dynamic' from which hybridity is formed. Indian art itself is offered as an index of the validity and success of a project of hybridisation. Zeeny Vakil as art critic seeks at the root of Indian art:

> an ethic of historically validated eclecticism, for was not the entire national culture based on the principle of borrowing whatever clothes seemed to fit, Aryan, Mughal, British, take-the-best-and-leave-the-rest? (*SV*, 52)

Interestingly, there is an echo of Brennan's criticism of *Grimus* here, the text which to him '"trie[d] on" cultures like used clothing'.[49] The criticism of that text is fair, but the importance for *The Satanic Verses* is that such a composite structure is here validated. *Grimus*'s structure operates like the quick-change artist who moves in and out of disparate and unrelated 'outfits', while Indian art, and alongside it, *The Satanic Verses*, displays its parti-coloured wardrobe and rejoices in its mismatches and eclecticism. Hind Sufiyan's famed cooking at the Shaandaar Café serves as a similar metaphor for such hybridity and eclecticism, her 'gastronomic pluralism' (*SV*, 246) representing the different influences upon her own 'art', western as well as eastern, as her husband recognises: '"and let us not pretend that Western culture is not present; after these centuries, how could it not also be part of our heritage?"' (*SV*, 246).

Related to this is Rushdie's refusal to subscribe to the concept of psychological as well as cultural purity. *The Satanic Verses* refutes the fallacy that the self can be '(ideally) homogeneous, non-hybrid, "pure"'. (*SV*, 427) To refuse the absolutism of purity in any guise is both to question the image of the self that is promoted in colonial literature and to argue for an identity and a form of literature to represent it that will eschew such certainties. *The Satanic Verses* offers a picture of 'Vilayet' that, in its labyrinthine construction, its casual brutalities and temptations, becomes a test of the solidity of migrant identity.

While England still uses images of an alien other to shore up a national identity for itself, the post-colonial subject is no longer passive in the face of such demonisation, but can define his or her own identity by a similar process of opposition; opposition to English racism and English responses. It is the project in which *The Satanic Verses* itself is engaged – to refute the insult of difference by embracing it.

The important factor is that the restoration of identity to the post-colonial subject is then affirmed, as it is for Saladin, by his return to India – by the acceptance of an unalienated self-image, a culture and nationality that defines rather than disrupts that self. In the midst of his channel-hopping, Saladin chances on an image that represents the hybridisation at work in Rushdie's writing as well as in Saladin's own life; an image that validates diversity within unity and sets the seal on his own process of rebirth and synthesis:

> There it palpably was, a chimera with roots, firmly planted in and growing out of a piece of English earth: a tree, he thought, capable of taking the place of the one his father had chopped down in a distant garden in another, incompatible world. If such a tree were possible, then so was he: he, too, could cohere, send down roots, survive. (*SV*, 406)

The Moor's Last Sigh: a postscript

THE publication of Rushdie's latest major work of fiction, *The Moor's Last Sigh*,[1] shortly before the manuscript of this study was completed, made it possible to include the relatively brief assessment of the text provided here. *The Moor's Last Sigh* has proved to be a work which, while reinforcing many of the imperatives of Rushdie's writing discussed throughout this study, also reflects the restrictions imposed on his writing by his current existence under the fatwa.

Midnight's Children saw Rushdie using memory as the tool for recovering his past in Bombay. With his reconstruction of the city in *The Moor's Last Sigh*, the reliance on memory becomes a personal and political necessity. Effectively exiled not only from the India of his birth but also from the active and engaged life that was such an important source of ideas in his earlier work, Rushdie has been obliged, more than ever, to construct an 'India of the mind'.[2] In an interview with Amrit Dhillon in *India Today*, Rushdie records that this is the first book he has written on a computer (perhaps explaining why he gives even more of a free rein to his verbal facility in this text) and the first he has written about India without first going there, obliging him instead to draw on information collected in journals and diaries compiled during previous visits.[3]

The resulting text is both a homage to the power of memory and also strangely flat – with the two-dimensionality of a largely cerebral reconstitution of 'reality'. The standard response of reviewers to the text has been to pile on the adjectives in an apparent attempt to counter its verbosity with their own. It is interesting that the ebullience and vivacity of the work invoked by critics is sometimes proposed in culinary terms – as if a diet of bland literary fare has been interrupted by the arrival of strong meat and Indian spices. Thus Victoria Glendinning calls it 'a feast for anyone with a strong literary digestion'[4] while James Wood finds it on occasion 'a little sickening'.[5]

The Bombay of *The Moor's Last Sigh* is rather different from that of *Midnight's Children*. It is a Bombay which hails its Portuguese colonial heritage and whose key inhabitants are from the Jewish and Christian minorities on the Malabar Coast of southern India. The identity of the text's hero, Moraes Zogoiby or the 'Moor', is a blend of Catholic, Jewish, Arabic/Spanish and contemporary Indian influences. His is truly the hybrid, mongrel self proclaimed throughout Rushdie's work. The fact that this hybridity is also depicted in religious terms allows Rushdie to comment on the rise of Hindu communalism in India which he sees as attempting to define a Hindu-identified Indianness to the exclusion of all other religious and cultural factors in the nation's make-up. Moorish Spain becomes the historical mirror of Nehru's secular, democratic India – the Catholic reconquest of the former in the fifteenth century pre-saging for Rushdie the contemporary Hindu threat to the latter.

The greater emphasis on religion as a mainspring of personal and national identity in *The Moor's Last Sigh* adds weight to the text's deployment of elements of Hindu mythology and mythical archetypes. The Moor sees himself engaged in detailing a tragi-comic contemporary reworking of the *Mahabharata*, with its own feuding family at the centre but with burlesque and buffoonery replacing the portentous actions of gods and men which comprise the founding myth of the nation (*MLS*, 352). Beyond this, the idea of *Bharat mata* or 'Mother India' – the myth of the nation as nurturing female – is itself explored in its different manifestations. Indira Gandhi identified herself with the nation for political purposes as her election slogan – 'India is Indira and Indira is India' – testifies. Indira is once again in the background of Rushdie's work, while he also invokes the famous 1957 film 'Mother India' in which the actress Nargis played a peasant woman at the other end of the social spectrum to Indira but also representative of the nation. The text's own alternative *Bharat mata* is the Moor's mother, the artist Aurora Zogoiby, with her paintings which serve as allegories of the changing face of India.

As the Moor himself puts it, 'Motherness… is a big idea in India, maybe our biggest: the land as mother, the mother as land, as the firm ground beneath our feet' (*MLS*, 137). The Moor's own stormy relationship with Aurora has its suggested historical parallel in that of Indira and her son Sanjay. With both the latter parties now dead, Rushdie has no fear of another libel suit from the former first lady of Indian politics, this time for his intimations of immorality within this close mother/son relationship. Indira, like Aurora, is the proof that 'protean Mother India… could turn monstrous' (*MLS*, 61). Rushdie goes further by interpolating the myth-life of the Zogoibys into the myth-life of the nation, with rumours that Aurora is Nehru's mistress and is loathed by Indira. Rushdie even uses quotation from one of Nehru's letters to Indira as a supposed letter from Nehru to Aurora to underline this idea (*MLS*, 117–18).

Aurora's art, as Peter Kemp points out, assumes the same symbolic status within the text as did Rani Harappa's embroidered shawls in *Shame*.[6] Aurora, like Rushdie beyond her, is obsessed with the 'mythic-romantic mode in which history, family, politics and fantasy [jostle] each other' (*MLS*, 203). Her paintings assume the status of allegories, reflecting the mood and preoccupations of the nation itself – developing from the Moor's birth in 1957 to the Emergency twenty years later and reaching their high point after the fall of Indira Gandhi before darkening again with the latter's political resurrection and the surge of Hindu fundamentalism in contemporary India. The Moor sees the work Aurora produces in the decade after Independence as troubled by the tension between realism and fantasy. Her artistic coterie is said to contain such committed social realists as Mulk Raj Anand and Saadat Hasan Manto, and yet she also experiences the lure of the fantastic. It is again a recurrence of a theme within *Midnight's Children* and much of Rushdie's fictional and non-fictional writing, the question of the best way of depicting 'reality'. The story of the da Gama/Zogoiby dynasty intertwines with the history of Moorish Spain, allowing Aurora, and Rushdie, to explore both the hybrid elements of India's history and to expand on the idea of the palimpsest as a model for this hybridity.

Aurora's artist friend Vasco Miranda paints the figure of the Sultan Boabdil, (the last Moorish prince of Andalusia who handed over the Alhambra to the Catholic monarchs Ferdinand and Isabella), over a commissioned portrait of Aurora and her son. Aurora later reworks the same idea, replacing the Moor Boabdil with her own son. Aurora's husband Abraham is reputedly descended from Boabdil's Spanish/Jewish mistress – so the paintings speak of familial as well as national hybridity, are indeed for the Moor attempts 'to create a romantic myth of the plural, hybrid nation… using Arab Spain to reimagine India' (*MLS*, 227). The Moor as subject is also aware of his own hybrid lineage as a 'jewholic-anonymous, a cathjew nut, a stewpot, a mongrel cur… Yessir: a real Bombay mix' (*MLS*, 104).

While *The Moor's Last Sigh* continues to privilege hybridity as both cultural model and textual strategy, the post-*Satanic Verses* Rushdie is obliged to concede the pitfalls of a limitlessly mongrelised and relativist position. Rushdie appears to have a joke at the expense of Homi Bhabha, arch-theorist of hybridity, when he gives a study of Aurora's art the title 'Imperso-Nation and Dis/Semi/Nation: Dialogics of Eclecticism and Interrogations of Authenticity in A.Z' (*MLS*, 329), recalling Bhabha's own discussion of Rushdie in his essay 'DissemiNation'.[7] *The Moor's Last Sigh* celebrates love as the ultimate expression of hybridity – 'the blending of spirits' (*MLS*, 289) as opposed to cultures – and yet the great love of the Moor's life, Uma Sarasvati, becomes living proof of the drawbacks of such an idea. Uma is effectively a sociopath, capable of adapting her personality and the 'truth' of her life according to will, utterly ruthless and amoral. The devilry produced by her multiple selves serves for the Moor as a rebuke to the 'pluralist philosophy on which we had all been raised' (*MLS*, 272).

Rushdie has himself voiced similar reservations about the

moral authority of multiplicity and pluralism in an interview with Maya Jaggi:

> I was interested to try to suggest there's a flip side to pluralism; the down side can be confusion, formlessness, chaos, a lack of vision or singleness of purpose. There are some very strong, monolithic, brutal views around, and sometimes those who have a clearer view get further.[8]

If hybridity as a political watchword is problematic, the text itself still maintains it as a structural precedent. There are again echoes of Desani's *All About H. Hatterr* in the idiosyncratic and Indianised English of the characters: 'Hate me don't hate me but, it is plain as the colours on your by-the-way-excuse-me too-horrible bush-shirt that a bad thing is growing quickly here' (*MLS*, 23). In broader narrative terms, strategies familiar in Rushdie's work from *Midnight's Children* onwards are redeployed. As with Saleem Sinai, the Moor is another physically disinte-grating narrator, 'possessed by a terror of running out of time' (*MLS*, 152), in this instance subject to a peculiar physiological malady which makes him age prematurely. As with Saleem, he likens himself to Scheherazade, prolonging his life until he can complete his narrative.

The same elements of oral storytelling are again forefronted by the first-person narrative, particularly the manipulation of narrative time ('I must not run ahead of my story'(*MLS*, 107)) and the personal, rhetorical aspects of the voice addressing us ('Enough, enough; away with this soap-box!') (*MLS*, 129). Beyond the Moor's own narrative, Rushdie appears to be conscious of the possible drawbacks of literary and artistic pyrotechnics which blazen their political agenda too forcefully. In defending his mother's hybrid artistic project, the Moor offers a defence against the high-velocity didacticism of Rushdie's own art:

> So, yes, there was a didacticism here, but what with the vivid surrealism of colouring and the dynamic acceleration of her brush, it was easy not to feel preached at, to revel in the carnival without listening to the barker, to dance to the music without caring for the message in the song. (MLS, 227)

But this willingness to accept the medium without the message could prove increasingly problematic for Rushdie should he continue to regard them as truly separable. The critical reception of *The Moor's Last Sigh* seems indeed able to 'revel in the carnival' of Rushdie's prose while perhaps remaining less than convinced by the barker's call. The laudable desire to express solidarity with a writer threatened with silence may lead to Rushdie being praised for his performance while the content of his work suffers.

To return to the way in which the text employs the skills of memory, remarked on at the beginning of this discussion, may also help to illustrate further false notes in *The Moor's Last Sigh* and explain why the text reads in so many instances like an inferior, because less engaged and less heartfelt, version of *Midnight's Children*. It is the difference between a text which derives from and is predicated on a living connection with the past and which foregrounds memory as the primary faculty of the migrant, and one which offers researched history and the fabrication of memory in its place. The Moor's Spanish/Jewish/Christian/Indian heritage appeals as an *idea* rather than a model of reality and its invented co-ordinates are a million miles away from the lived experience which invests the pages of *Midnight's Children*.

The fact that *The Moor's Last Sigh* is the first instance of Rushdie consistently employing his own work as an intertext seems to reinforce this idea. There are reappearances for Shiva and Parvati's son Aadam, Lord Khusro Khusrovand and Commander Sabarmati from *Midnight's Children* and Zeeny Vakil from *The Satanic Verses*. The Bombay of *Midnight's Children* is obviously at the forefront of the text, with snapshots of Saleem's childhood landscape forming part of the panorama, while the idea of Bombay as 'the ocean of stories' (*MLS*, 350) recalls *Haroun*. This is a kind of 'second order' memory – distanced from the palpable 'reality' of *Midnight's Children* with its vivid evocation of the texture of the city, redeploying instead elements of that earlier landscape to give depth to a narrative played out largely behind closed doors.

A further criticism derives from the choice of love as the ultimate manifestation of hybridity in the text. Love may exhibit a defiance of purity and singularity, but as a model it illustrates something of a shift in emphasis from the political to the personal as the focus of interest for Rushdie. The political is still in evidence in *The Moor's Last Sigh*, but the Moor himself is not handcuffed to history in the way Saleem was, nor even as implicated in the political life of his nation as was Omar Khayyam Shakil in *Shame*. Aurora's involvement with Nehru is tangential to the narrative and the political affiliations of different characters are used more as reflections of aspects of their personalities (Camöens's idealism, Aires's conservatism) than as a focus for political debate.

This has a tendency to make the text read like a series of set pieces or cameos on hybridity, art, politics and love affairs rather than as a seamless and organic whole. Characters become too representative of ideas or positions to be wholly engaging or sympathetic. Women are again 'centre stage' as so often in Rushdie's work, but the ambivalence towards them evident in earlier texts is here equally apparent. Violent or grisly deaths are the lot of most of the text's female players – with Aurora murdered, her three daughters dying of cancer, chemical poisoning and terrorist attack respectively, Uma dying by her own hand, and even bit-player Zeeny Vakil being blown up. Nadia Wadia – former Miss India – escapes lightly in comparison, with her beauty permanently disfigured. The theme of the blurring of the real and mythical status of women in India is indistinguishable from the same impulse in Rushdie's own characterisations. Uma, whose name recalls the incarnation of the Mother goddess in Hinduism, becomes also a manifestation of Kali, a goddess of destruction desiring men's souls, like the 'Black Widow' Indira before her, to sustain her.

A largely negative assessment of Rushdie's latest major work may appear churlish when viewed against the circumstances of its production, but it would be wrong to allow Rushdie's situation to engender a sycophantic suspension of critical judgement in the face of *The Moor's Last Sigh*'s problematic elements. Many of those problems, as has been suggested, appear to derive from the author's now wholly real rather than largely metaphorical status as 'exile'. The forthright personal and political agendas which have always informed Rushdie's writing mean that he will need to be returned to the world if he is to fully recapture the bombastic dynamism of his best work.

Notes

Chapter 1

1 Salman Rushdie, *The Satanic Verses*, (London, Viking/Penguin, 1988), p. 8.

2 Salman Rushdie, 'In Good Faith', in *Imaginary Homelands: Essays and and Criticism 1981–1991*, (London, Granta, 1991), p. 394.

3 'An Interview with Salman Rushdie', *Scripsi*, 3:2/3 (1985), p. 124.

4 Homi K. Bhabha, 'Signs Taken for Wonders: Questions of Ambivalence and Authority, Under a Tree Outside Delhi, May 1917' in *Europe and Its Others*, F. Barker *et al.*,(eds), (Colchester, University of Essex, 1985), p. 100.

5 John Haffenden, (ed.), *Novelists in Interview*, (London, Methuen, 1985) pp. 233–4.

6 Homi K. Bhabha, *The Location of Culture*, (London, Routledge, 1994), p. 225.

7 Salman Rushdie, *Shame*, (London, Jonathan Cape, 1983), p. 29.

8 Anuradha Dingwaney Needham, 'Author(iz)ing *Midnight's Children* and *Shame*: Salman Rushdie's Constructions of Authority' in Emmanuel S. Nelson (ed.), *Reworlding: the Literature of the Indian Diaspora*, (Westport CT, Greenwood Press, 1992), p. 159. See also Srinivas Aravamudan, '"Being God's Postman is no Fun, Yaar"', *Diacritics*, 19:2 (1989), 3–20 for discussion of filmic intertexts in *The Satanic Verses*.

9 Haffenden, *Novelists in Interview*, p. 247.

10 Salman Rushdie, *East, West*, (London, Jonathan Cape, 1994), p. 186.

11 *Mahabharata*, trans. C. Rajagopalachari, (Bombay, Bharitya Vidya Bhavan, 1955), p. 91.

12   Sara Suleri, *The Rhetoric of English India*, (Chicago, Chicago UP, 1992), p. 191.

13   Timothy Brennan, *Salman Rushdie and the Third World: Myths of the Nation*, (London, Macmillan, 1989).

14   Aadam Aziz experiences this loss in Salman Rushdie, *Midnight's Children*, (London, Picador, 1982), p. 10. Rushdie discusses his own ungodliness in 'Is Nothing Sacred?', *Imaginary Homelands*, p. 417.

15   *Scripsi* interview, p. 116.

16   See for example Carter's *Wise Children*, (London, Vintage, 1991), p. 11.

17   See for example *Scripsi* interview, p. 116. An extended discussion of Rushdie's relation to magical realism can be found in the Critical Overview in this study.

18   Salman Rushdie, '*Midnight's Children* and *Shame*', *Kunapipi*, 7:1 (1985), 7.

19   See discussion of *Haroun* and also Jean-Pierre Durix, '"The Gardener of Stories": Salman Rushdie's *Haroun and the Sea of Stories*', *Journal of Commonwealth Literature*, 29:1 (1993), 114–22.

20   See chapter on *Midnight's Children*.

21   The term 'Indo-Anglian' is here used to refer to Indian writing in English.

22   Raja Rao, Foreword to *Kanthapura*, (New York, New Directions, 1963), p. vii.

23   Mulk Raj Anand, 'Pigeon Indian: Some Notes on Indian-English Writing', *World Literature Written in English*, 21, Spring, (1982), 325–36.

24   Anand, 'Some Notes', p. 328.

25   *Scripsi* interview, p. 124.

26   This observation was made by the Indo-Anglian novelist Upamanyu Chatterjee, interviewed by Catherine Cundy, University of Kent, 5 December 1991.

27   *Scripsi* interview, p. 118.

28   Rao, Foreword to *Kanthapura*, p. viii.

29   Salman Rushdie, 'The Empire Writes Back with a Vengeance', *The Times*, 3 July 1982, p. 8.

30   G. V. Desani, *All About H. Hatterr*, (Harmondsworth, Penguin, 1982), p. 37.

31   Desani, *All About*, p. 35.

32   Rushdie, 'The Empire Writes Back', p. 8.

33   Raja Rao, Foreword to *Kanthapura*, p. viii.

34   M. D. Fletcher (ed.), *Reading Rushdie: Perspectives on the Fiction of Salman Rushdie*, (Amsterdam, Rodopi, 1994), pp. 1–22.

35   *Kunapipi* (1985), 17.

36   *Ibid.*

37   Richard Cronin, *Imagining India*, (London, Macmillan, 1989), pp. 46–7.

38   See for example his introduction to *Home Front*, Derek Bishton and John Reardon, (London, Jonathan Cape, 1984), pp. 6–7.

39   See his article 'Bosnia on My Mind', *Index on Censorship*, 22, 1–2, May–June, pp. 16–20.

40   See the narrator's comments in *Shame*, p. 22.

Chapter 2

1   See L. Appignanesi and S. Maitland (eds), *The Rushdie File*, (London, Fourth Estate, 1989), p. 3.

2   See Uma Parameswaran on word-play in *Grimus* in *The Perforated Sheet: Essays in Salman Rushdie's Art*, (New Delhi, Affiliated East–West, 1988), pp. 55–66.

3   Timothy Brennan, *Salman Rushdie and the Third World: Myths of the Nation*, (London, Macmillan, 1989), p. 70.

4   Frantz Fanon, *The Wretched of the Earth*, (Harmondsworth, Penguin, 1967), p. 168.

5   Fanon, *Wretched*, pp. 176–7.

6   Brennan, *Salman Rushdie*, p. 71.

7   Salman Rushdie, *Grimus*, (London, Grafton, 1989), p. 17.

8   *Rasselas* in *Samuel Johnson*, Donald Greene (ed.), Oxford Authors, (Oxford, OUP, 1984), p. 340.

9   Dorothy L. Sayers, 'Introduction' to Dante Alighieri, *Purgatory*, (Harmondsworth, Penguin, 1955), p. 69.

10   'An Interview with Salman Rushdie', *Scripsi* 3:2/3 (1985), p. 125.

11   Farid ud-Din 'Attar, *Conference of the Birds*, trans. S. C. Nott, (London, Janus, 1954), p. 12.

12   'Attar', *Conference*, p. 131.

13 Brennan, *Salman Rushdie*, p. 72.

14 Laleh Bakhtiar, *Sufi: Expressions of the Mystic Quest*, (London, Thames & Hudson, 1976), pp. 27–8.

15 Brennan, *Salman Rushdie*, p. 77.

16 Ib Johansen, 'The Flight from the Enchanter: Reflections on Salman Rushdie's *Grimus*', *Kunapipi*, 7:1 (1985), 20–32.

17 Mikhail Bakhtin, *Problems of Dostoevsky's Poetics*, Caryl Emerson trans. and ed., (Manchester, MUP, 1984), p. 114.

18 Bakhtin, *Problems*, pp. 116–17.

19 *Scripsi* interview, p. 125.

20 Eric S. Rabkin, *The Fantastic in Literature*, (Princeton NJ, Princeton UP, 1976), p. 121.

21 Eric S. Rabkin (ed.), *Science Fiction: A Historical Anthology*, (New York, OUP, 1983), p. 4.

22 *Scripsi* interview, p. 125.

Chapter 3

1 'An Interview with Salman Rushdie', *Scripsi* 3:2/3 (1985), p. 125.

2 Salman Rushdie, '*Midnight's Children* and *Shame*', *Kunapipi*, 7:1 (1985), 6.

3 Rushdie cites these influences in numerous places, among them 'Salman Rushdie', *Kunapipi*, 4:2 (1982), 20; *Scripsi* interview, p. 115 and *Imaginary Homelands*, p. 21.

4 Walter J. Ong, *Orality and Literacy: The Technologizing of the Word*, (New York, Routledge, 1982).

5 Ong, *Orality*, p. 144.

6 See Rushdie interview with Chandrabhan Pattanayak in *The Literary Criterion*, 18:3 (1983), 20.

7 Nancy E. Batty, 'The Art of Suspense: Rushdie's 1001 (Mid-) Nights', *Ariel*, 18:3 (1987), 49–65.

8 Roland Barthes, 'The Death of the Author', *Image Music Text*, S. Heath trans., (London, Collins, 1977), p. 148.

9 Batty, 'The Art of Suspense', p. 54.

10 *Ibid.*, p. 56.

11 Ong, Orality, p. 101.

12 Rushdie interview with James Fenton, 'Keeping Up with Salman Rushdie' *New York Review of Books*, 28 March 1991, p. 31.

13 Keith Wilson, '*Midnight's Children* and Reader Responsibility', *Critical Quarterly*, 26:3 (1984), 27.

14 Timothy Brennan, *Salman Rushdie and the Third World: Myths of the Nation*, (London, Macmillan, 1989), p. 116.

15 *Kunapipi* (1985), 3.

16 Ved Mehta, *A Family Affair: India Under Three Prime Ministers*, (New York, OUP, 1982), p. 26.

17 Larry Collins and Domonique Lapierre, *Freedom at Midnight*, (London, Collins, 1975), pp. 70–1.

18 Collins and Lapierre, *Freedom*, p. 168.

19 Benedict Anderson, *Imagined Communities: Reflections on the Origins and Spread of Nationalism*, (London, Verso, 1983).

20 I am grateful to Katherine Frank for sight of the manuscript of her article 'Mr Rushdie and Mrs Gandhi' to be published in *Biography* in 1997.

21 *Kunapipi* (1982), 19.

22 Ashis Nandy, 'Satyajit Ray's Secret Guide', *East–West Film Journal*, 4:2 (1990), 15.

23 See Nayantara Sahgal, 'The Schizophrenic Imagination' in S. Chew and A. Rutherford (eds), *Unbecoming Daughters of the Empire*, (Sydney, Dangaroo, 1993), p. 115.

24 Witness critical responses to the text's publication such as 'India has found her Günter Grass', reproduced on the cover of the 1982 Picador edition of the text.

25 *Kunapipi* (1985), 6.

Chapter 4

1 Peter Brigg, 'Salman Rushdie's Novels: The Disorder in Fantastic Order', *World Literature Written in English*, 27:1 (1987), 119.

2 'Benazir.... does not correspond to Iskander Harappa's daughter in *Shame*.' Salman Rushdie, '*Midnight's Children* and *Shame*', *Kunapipi*, 7:1 (1985), 18. 'To say that Arjumand Harappa is Benazir Bhutto is nonsense, she isn't, that was never the intention.' 'An Interview with Salman Rushdie', *Scripsi* 3:2/3 (1985), p. 108.

3   Salman Rushdie, *The Jaguar Smile: A Nicaraguan Journey*, (London, Pan, 1987), p. 146.

4   *Scripsi* interview, 108.

5   *Kunapipi* (1985), 18.

6   *Kunapipi*, Salman Rushdie', 4:2 (1982), 26.

7   *Kunapipi* (1985), 15–16.

8   *Ibid.*, 13.

9   I adopt James Kritzeck's spelling of the name in his *Anthology of Islamic Literature*, (Harmondsworth, Penguin, 1964), p. 179 to help distinguish between the poet and Rushdie's creation.

10 Kritzeck, *Anthology*, p. 278.

11 Amitav Ghosh, *The Shadow Lines*, (London, Black Swan, 1989), p. 27.

12 *Scripsi* interview, p. 110.

13 Anuradha Dingwaney Needham, 'The Politics of Post-Colonial Identity in Salman Rushdie', *Massachusetts Review*, 29:4 (1988/9), 624.

14 Timothy Brennan, *Salman Rushdie and the Third World: Myths of the Nation*, (London, Macmillan, 1989), p. 126

15 From the *Rubaiyyat* of Umar Khayyam, trans. E. Fitzgerald, in Kritzeck, *Anthology*, p. 180.

16 Aijaz Ahmad, *In Theory: Classes, Nations, Literatures*, (London, Verso, 1992), p. 148.

17 Ahmad, *In Theory*, p. 144.

18 Salman Rushdie in conversation with Günter Grass in *Voices: Writers and Politics*, B. Browne, U. Eichter and D. Herman (eds), (Nottingham, Spokesman, 1987), p. 63.

19 Dingwaney Needham, *Massachusetts Review*, 617.

20 Fredric Jameson, 'Third World Literature in the Era of Multinational Capitalism', *Social Text*, 15, Fall (1986), 65–88.

21 Aijaz Ahmad, 'Jameson's Rhetoric of Otherness and the "National Allegory"', *Social Text*, 17, Fall (1987), 5.

22 Ahmad, *Social Text*, 7.

23 Brennan, *Rushdie*, pp. 70, 105, 139 and 154.

24 Jameson, *Social Text*, 73.

25 *Ibid.*, 69.

26 Gay Clifford, *The Transformations of Allegory*, (London, RKP, 1974), p. 5.

27 Jameson, *Social Text*, 83.

28 Clifford, *Transformations*, p. 29.

29 *Ibid.*, 45.

30 *Scripsi* interview, p. 108.

31 *Kunapipi* (1985), 18.

Chapter 5

1 It is interesting to note that Malise Ruthven's account of the 'Rushdie affair' changed its title between hardback and paperback editions. The subtitle of *A Satanic Affair: Salman Rushdie and the Rage of Islam* was amended for the 1991 Hogarth Press reprint to *Salman Rushdie and the Wrath of Islam*, apparently conceding at least an element of control in the anger of Muslims towards Rushdie's text.

2 James Fenton in the interview 'Keeping Up with Salman Rushdie', *New York Review of Books*, 28, March 1991, refers to just such a falling-out when he quotes the comments of lawyer Francis Bennion on resigning from the Salman Rushdie Defence Committee.

3 Maxime Rodinson, *Mohammed*, trans. A. Carter, (London, Allen Lane, 1971), p. 56

4 N. J. Dawood, translation with notes of *The Koran*, (Harmondsworth, Penguin, 1990), p. ix.

5 Rodinson, *Mohammed*, p. 107.

6 Accounts of these events are offered by, among others, Rodinson, pp. 106–7; James Kritzeck in *Anthology of Islamic Literature*, (Harmondsworth, Penguin, 1964), p. 38 and W. J. Weatherby in *Salman Rushdie: Sentenced to Death*, (New York, Carroll & Graf, 1990), p. 26.

7 *The Koran*, p. 525.

8 Prafulla Mohanti in *Through Brown Eyes*, (Oxford, OUP, 1985), p. 1 describes the Indian reverence for 'Bilayat' and anything 'Bilayati'.

9 V. S. Naipaul, *The Enigma of Arrival: A Novel in Five Sections*, (Harmondsworth: Penguin, 1987), p. 57.

10 V. S. Naipaul, *An Area of Darkness*, (Harmondsworth, Penguin, [1964] 1970), p. 57.

11   Nicholas D. Rombes Jr., 'The Satanic Verses as Cinematic Narrative', Literature/Film Quarterly, 11:1 (1993), 48.

12   Ibid., 53.

13   Bharati Mukherjee, Jasmine, (London, Virago, [1988] 1991).

14   Prafulla Mohanti also attests to the totemic significance of the A–Z in Through Brown Eyes, p. 33.

15   Naipaul, An Area of Darkness, p. 201.

16   Gayatri C. Spivak, 'Reading The Satanic Verses', Third Text, 11, Summer (1990), 49.

17   Salman Rushdie, interview with Mark Lawson, 'Fishing for Salman', The Independent, 10 September 1988, p. 62.

18   Franz Fanon, The Wretched of the Earth (Harmondsworth, Penguin, 1967), p. 201.

19   Ashis Nandy, The Intimate Enemy: Loss and Recovery of Self Under Colonialism, (Delhi, OUP, 1983), p. 107.

20   Ibid., p. 109.

21   Timothy Brennan, Salman Rushdie and the Third World: Myths of the Nation, (London, Macmillan, 1989), p. 126

22   Malise Ruthven, Salman Rushdie and the Wrath of Islam, (London, Hogarth Press, 1991), pp. 21 and 23.

23   Janet Frame, The Envoy from Mirror City: An Autobiography, Vol. 3, (New Zealand, Century Hutchinson, 1985), p. 10.

24   Philip Engblom, 'A Multitude of Voices: Carnivalization and Dialogocality in the Novels of Salman Rushdie' in M. D. Fletcher (ed.), Reading Rushdie: Perspectives on the Fiction of Salman Rushdie, Cross Cultures 16, Amsterdam, Rodopi, 1994, p. 301.

25   Carlos Fuentes, The Guardian, 24 February 1989, quoted in The Rushdie File, pp. 245–6.

Chapter 6

1   Rushdie interview with James Fenton, 'Keeping Up with Salman Rushdie', New York Review of Books, 28 March 1991, p. 31

2   Ibid., p. 32.

3   Salman Rushdie, The Wizard of Oz: A Short Text About Magic, BFI Film Classics (London, BFI, 1992), p. 9.

4   Fenton, 'Keeping Up', p. 32.

5   *Ibid.*, p. 31.

6   Salman Rushdie, *Haroun and the Sea of Stories*, (London, Granta, 1990), p. 22.

7   Kenneth Cragg, *The Call of the Minaret*, (London, Collins, 1986), p. 123, my emphases.

8   See Vasanti Joshi, 'Sea Trade as Depicted in *The Kathasaritsagara*', *Journal of the Oriental Institute*, 36:1–4 (1986/7), 171.

9   Roland Barthes, 'The Death of the Author', *Image Music Text*, S. Heath trans., (London, Collins, 1977), p. 146.

10 Salman Rushdie interview with Sara Rance, *The Observer*, 3 May 1992, p. 54.

11 'An Interview with Salman Rushdie', *Scripsi* 3:2/3 (1985), p. 116.

12 Fenton, 'Keeping Up', p. 32.

13 Upendrakishore Ray Chaudhuri, 'The Adventures of Goopy and Bagha' in *Noon in Calcutta: Short Stories from Bengal*, K. Dutta and A. Robinson (eds), (London, Bloomsbury, 1992), pp. 51–65.

Chapter 7

1   M. D. Fletcher, 'Salman Rushdie: An Annotated Bibliography', *Journal of Indian Writing in English*, 19:1 (1991), 15–23.

2   Colin Smith, 'The Unbearable Lightness of Salman Rushdie', in D. Riemenschneider (ed.), *Critical Approaches to the New Literatures in English*, (Essen, Blaue Eule, 1989), pp. 104–15.

3   M. Keith Booker, '*Finnegan's Wake* and *The Satanic Verses*: Two Modern Myths of the Fall', *Critique*, 32:3 (1991), 190–207.

4   Patricia Merivale, 'Saleem Fathered by Oscar: Intertextual Strategies in *Midnight's Children* and *The Tin Drum*', *Ariel*, 21:3 (1990), 5–21.

5   Wimal Dissanayake, 'Towards a Decolonized English: South Asian Creativity in Fiction', *World Englishes*, 4:2 (1985), 233–42.

6   Ron Shepherd, '*Midnight's Children*: The Parody of an Indian Novel', *SPAN*, 21 (1985), 184–92.

7   Sara Suleri, *The Rhetoric of English India*, (Chicago, Chicago UP, 1992).

8   Uma Parameswaran, *The Perforated Sheet: Essays in Salman Rushdie's Art* (New Delhi, Affiliated East–West, 1988).

9   David W. Price, 'Salman Rushdie's "Use and Abuse of History" in *Midnight's Children*', Ariel, 25:2 (1994), 91–107.

10   David Birch, 'Postmodernist Chutneys', *Textual Practice*, 5:1 (1991), 1–7.

11   Srinivas Aravamudan, 'Being God's Postman is No Fun, Yaar', *Diacritics* 19:2 (1989), 3–20.

12   Timothy Brennan, *Salman Rushdie and the Third World: Myths of the Nation*, (London, Macmillan, 1989).

13   *Ibid.*, p. 166.

14   *Ibid.*, p. 141.

15   James Harrison, *Salman Rushdie*, Twaynes English Authors Series, (New York, Twayne, 1992), p. 128.

16   Malise Ruthven, *A Satanic Affair: Salman Rushdie and the Wrath of Islam*, (London, Hogarth, 1990).

17   L. Appignanesi and S. Maitland (eds), *The Rushdie File*, (London, Fourth Estate, 1989).

18   W. J. Weatherby, *Salman Rushdie: Sentenced to Death* (New York, Carroll and Graf, 1990).

19   Dan Cohn-Sherbok (ed.), *The Salman Rushdie Controversy in Inter-Religious Perspective*, (Lampeter, Edwin Mellen, 1990).

20   Margaret Drabble (ed.), *Oxford Companion to English Literature*, 5th. edn, (Oxford, OUP, 1985), p. 855.

21   Homi K. Bhabha, introduction to Bhabha (ed.), *Nation and Narration*, (London, Routledge, 1990), p. 7.

22   Jean-Pierre Durix, 'Magic Realism in *Midnight's Children*', *Commonwealth Essays and Studies*, 8:1 (1985) 57.

23   Aija Ahmad, *In Theory: Classes, Nations, Literatures*, (London, Verso, 1992), p. 69.

24   Salman Rushdie, interview with Mark Lawson, 'Fishing for Salman', *The Independent*, 10 September 1988, p.60.

25   Salman Rushdie, '*Midnight's Children* and *Shame*', *Kunapipi*, 7:1 (1985), 15.

26   Cora Kaplan, 'The Feminist Politics of Literary Theory', in *Ideas from France* (London, ICA Documents, 1985), p. 33.

27   Jean-François Lyotard, *The Postmodern Condition: A Report on Knowledge*, G. Bennington and B. Massumi trans., (Manchester, MUP, 1984), p. xxiv.

28   Linda Hutcheon, A *Poetics of Postmodernism: History, Theory, Fiction*, (New York, Routledge, 1988), p. 5.

29   Fredric Jameson, 'Postmodernism and Consumer Society' in Hal Foster (ed.), *Postmodern Culture*, (London, Pluto, 1987), p. 114.

30   Jean Baudrillard, 'The Ecstasy of Communication', in Foster (ed.), *Postmodern Culture*, p. 132.

31   *Ibid.*

32   Jorge Luis Borges, 'The Garden of Forking Paths' in D. A. Yates and J. E. Irby (eds), *Labyrinths: Selected Stories and Other Writings*, (Harmondsworth, Penguin, 1970), p. 50.

33   Wendy B. Faris, *Labyrinths of Language:Symbolic Landscape and Narrative Design in Modern Fiction*, (Baltimore, Johns Hopkins UP, 1988), p. 12.

34   Baudrillard, 'The Ecstasy', pp. 126–7.

35   *Ibid.*, p. 127.

36   M. D. Fletcher (ed.), *Reading Rushdie, Perspectives on the Fiction of Salman Rushdie*, (Amsterdam, Rodopi, 1994), p. 8.

37   Salman Rushdie interview with David Brooks in *Helix*, 19 (1984), 56.

38   *Ibid.*, p. 57.

39   For a further discussion of this issue see Catherine Cundy, 'Rushdie's Women', *Wasafiri*, 18 (1993), 13–17.

40   Ahmad, *In Theory*, p. 144.

41   Inderpal Grewal, 'Marginality, Women and *Shame*', *Genders*, 3 (1988), 37.

42   Anuradha Dingwaney Needham, 'The Politics of Post-Colonial Identity in Salman Rushdie', *Massachusetts Review*, 29:4 (1988/9), 614.

43   Homi K. Bhabha, 'DissemiNation' in *Nation and Narration*, p. 318.

44   Homi K. Bhabha, 'Representation and the Colonial Text: A Critical Exploration of Some Forms of Mimeticism' in Frank Gloversmith (ed.), *The Theory of Reading*, (Brighton, Harvester, 1984), pp. 93–122.

45   B. Ashcroft, G. Griffiths, H. Tiffin, *The Empire Writes Back: Theory and Practice in Post-Colonial Literatures*, (London, Routledge, 1989), p. 184.

46   *Ibid.*, p. 185.

47   B. Ashcroft, G. Griffiths and H. Tiffin (eds), *The Post-Colonial Studies Reader*, (London, Routledge, 1995), p. 184.

48   *Ibid.*

49   Brennan, *Salman Rushdie*, p. 71.

Chapter 8

1   Salman Rushdie, *The Moor's Last Sigh*, (London, Jonathan Cape, 1995).

2   Rushdie writes in his essay 'Imaginary Homelands' that writers who look back at the past will inevitably 'create fictions, not actual cities or villages, but invisible ones, imaginary homelands, Indias of the mind', *Imaginary Homelands*, p. 10.

3   Rushdie interview with Amrit Dhillon, *India Today*, 10 September 1995, p. 138.

4   Victoria Glendinning, 'An Unsuitable Boy's Literary Feast', *The Daily Telegraph*, 2 September 1995, p. 6.

5   James Wood, 'Tales from the Lost City', *The Guardian*, 8 September 1995, p. 5.

6   Peter Kemp, 'Absolutely Fabulous', *The Sunday Times*, 3 September 1995, p. 2.

7   Homi K. Bhabha, 'DissemiNation' in Bhabha (ed.), *Nation and Narration*, (London, Routledge, 1990), pp. 291–322.

8   Rushdie interview with Maya Jaggi, *New Statesman and Society*, 8 September 1995, p. 21.

Select bibliography

Primary

BOOKS BY RUSHDIE

Grimus, London, Grafton, [1975] 1989.

Midnight's Children, London, Picador, [1981] 1982.

Shame, London, Jonathan Cape, 1983.

The Jaguar Smile: A Nicaraguan Journey, London, Picador, 1987.

The Satanic Verses, London, Viking/Penguin, 1988.

Haroun and the Sea of Stories, London, Granta, 1990.

Imaginary Homelands: Essays and Criticism 1981–1991, London, Granta, 1991.

The Wizard of Oz: A Short Text About Magic, BFI Film Classics, London, BFI, 1992.

East, West, London, Jonathan Cape, 1994.

The Moor's Last Sigh, London, Jonathan Cape, 1995.

ARTICLES, ESSAYS AND INTERVIEWS BY RUSHDIE

Interview with Victoria Glendinning, *The Sunday Times*, 25 October 1981, p. 38.

The Empire Writes Back with a Vengeance, *The Times*, 3 July 1982. p.8. (Reprinted in IH, 129–138)

'Angel Gabriel', (review of Márquez's *Chronicle of a Death Foretold*), *London Review of Books*, 16 September 1982, pp. 3–4. (Reprinted as 'Gabriel García Márquez' in *IH*, 299–305)

'Imaginary Homelands', *London Review of Books*, 20 October 1982, pp. 18–19. (Reprinted in *IH*, 9–21)

'Salman Rushdie', *Kunapipi*, 4:2 (1982), 17–26.

'The Indian Writer in England', in Maggie Butcher (ed.), *The Eye of the Beholder: Essays on Indian Writing*, London, Commonwealth Institute, 1983, pp. 75–83.

Interview with Chandrabhanu Pattanayak, *Literary Criterion*, 18:3 (1983), 19–22.

Interview with David Brooks, *Helix*, 19 (1984), 55–69.

'"Errata" or Unreliable Narration in *Midnight's Children*' in B. Olinder (ed.), *A Sense of Place: Essays in Post-Colonial Literatures*, Gothenburg, Gothenburg University Commonwealth Studies, 1984, pp. 98–100. (Reprinted in *IH*, 22–5)

'Outside the Whale' *Granta*, 11 (1984), 125–138. (Reprinted in *IH*, 87–101)

'An Interview with Salman Rushdie', *Scripsi*, 3:2/3 (1985), 107–26.

'*Midnight's Children* and *Shame*', *Kunapipi*, 7:1 (1985), 1–19.

Interview with John Haffenden in Haffenden (ed.), *Novelists in Interview*, London, Methuen, 1985, pp. 231–61.

Conversation with Günter Grass in B. Bourne, U. Eichter and D. Herman (eds), *Voices: Writers and Politics*, Nottingham, Spokesman, 1987.

'Zia Unmourned' *Nation*, 19 September 1988, pp. 188–9. (Reprinted as 'Zia ul-Haq, 17 August 1988' in *IH*, 53–55)

'Fishing for Salman', interview with Mark Lawson, *The Independent*, 10 September 1988, pp. 58–62.

'In Good Faith', *The Independent on Sunday*, 4 February 1990. (Reprinted in *IH*, 393–414).

Is Nothing Sacred?', The Herbert Read Memorial Lecture, 6 February 1990, London, Granta, 1990. (Reprinted in *IH*, 415–29)

'Homage to Satyajit Ray', *London Review of Books*, 8 March 1990, p. 9. (Reprinted as 'Satyajit Ray' in *IH*, 107–14)

'Keeping up with Salman Rushdie', interview with James Fenton, *New York Review of Books*, 28 March 1991, pp. 24–32.

Interview with Sara Rance, *Observer*, 3 May 1992, p. 54.

'Bosnia on My Mind,' *Index on Censorship*, 22:1/2 (1994), 16–20.

Secondary

SELECTED RUSHDIE CRITICISM

Ahmad, A., 'Salman Rushdie's *Shame*: Postmodern Migrancy and the Representation of Women', in Ahmad, *In Theory: Classes, Nations, Literatures*, London, Verso, 1992, pp. 123–58.

Aravamudan, S., 'Being God's Postman is No Fun, Yaar', *Diacritics*, 19:2 (1989), 3–20.

Batty, N., 'The Art of Suspense: Rushdie's 1001 (Mid-Nights)', *Ariel*, 18:3 (1987), 49–65.

Birch, D., 'Postmodernist Chutneys,' *Textual Practice*, 5:1 (1991), 1–7.

Booker, M. K., '*Finnegan's Wake* and *The Satanic Verses*: Two Modern Myths of the Fall', *Critique*, 32:3 (1991), 190–207.

Brennan, T., *Salman Rushdie and the Third World: Myths of the Nation*, London, Macmillan, 1989.

Couto, M., 'Midnight's Children and Parents: The Search for Indo-British Identity', *Encounter*, 58:2 (1982), 61–6.

Cronin, R., *Imagining India*, London, Macmillan, 1989.

Cundy, C., 'Rehearsing Voices: Salman Rushdie's *Grimus*', *Journal of Commonwealth Literature*, 27:1 (1992), 128–38.

Cundy, C., 'Rushdie's Women', *Wasafiri*, 18 (1993), 13–17.

Dingwaney Needham, A., 'The Politics of Post-Colonial Identity in Salman Rushdie', *Massachusetts Review*, 29:4 (1988/9), 609–24.

Dissanayake, W., 'Towards a Decolonized English: South Asian Creativity in Fiction', *World Englishes*, 4:2 (1985), 233–42.

Durix, J.-P., 'Magic Realism in *Midnight's Children*', *Commonwealth Essays and Studies*, 8:1 (1985), 57–63.

Durix, J.-P., '"The Gardener of Stories": Salman Rushdie's *Haroun and the Sea of Stories*,' *Journal of Commonwealth Literature*, 29:1 (1993), 114–22.

Engblom, P., 'A Multitude of Voices: Carnivalization and Dialogicality in the Novels of Salman Rushdie,' in M. D. Fletcher (ed.) *Reading Rushdie: Perspectives on the Fiction of Salman Rushdie*, Cross/Cultures 16, Amsterdam, Rodopi, 1994, pp. 293–304.

Fletcher, M. D., 'Rushdie's *Shame* as Apologue', *Journal of Commonwealth Literature*, 21:1 (1986), 120–32.

Fletcher, M. D. (ed.), *Reading Rushdie: Perspectives on the Fiction of Salman Rushdie*, Cross/Cultures 16, Amsterdam, Rodopi, 1994.

Grewal, I., 'Salman Rushdie: Marginality, Women and *Shame*', *Genders*, 16:2 (1988), 210–227.

Harrison, J., *Salman Rushdie*, Twaynes English Authors Series, New York, Twayne, 1992.

Johansen, I., 'The Flight from the Enchanter: Reflections on Salman Rushdie's *Grimus*', *Kunapipi*, 7:1 (1985), 20–32.

Merivale, P., 'Saleem Fathered by Oscar: Intertextual Strategies in *Midnight's Children* and *The Tin Drum*,' *Ariel*, 21:3 (1990), 5–21.

Parameswaran, U., *The Perforated Sheet: Essays in Salman Rushdie's Art*, New Delhi, Affiliated East–West, 1988.

Price, D. W., 'Salman Rushdie's "Use and Abuse of History" in *Midnight's Children*', *Ariel*, 25:2 (1994), 91–107.

Rombes Jr., N., '*The Satanic Verses* as Cinematic Narrative', *Literature/Film Quarterly*, 11:1 (1993), 47–53.

Shepherd, R., '*Midnight's Children*: The Parody of an Indian Novel', *SPAN*, 21 (1985), 184–92.

Smith, C., 'The Unbearable Lightness of Salman Rushdie', in D. Riemenschneider (ed.), *Critical Approaches to the New Literatures in English*, Essen, Blaue Eule, 1989, pp. 104–15.

Spivak, G., 'Reading *The Satanic Verses*', *Third Text*, 11 (1990), 41–60.

Suleri, S., 'Salman Rushdie: Embodiments of Blasphemy, Censorships of Shame', in Suleri, T*he Rhetoric of English India*, Chicago, Chicago UP, 1992, pp. 174–206.

Wilson, K., '*Midnight's Children* and Reader Responsibility', *Critical Quarterly*, 26:3 (1984), 23–37.

Index